Magazines for Kids and Teens

Revised Edition

Donald R. Stoll

Editor

Educational Press Association of America
Rowan College of New Jersey
201 Mullica Hill Road
Glassboro, New Jersey 08028-1701, USA

International Reading Association
800 Barksdale Road, PO Box 8139
Newark, Delaware 19714-8139, USA

The publishers welcome any information that will lead to correction or clarification of such information in future printings.

Director of Publications   Joan M. Irwin
Assistant Director of Publications   Wendy Lapham Russ
Senior Editor   Christian A. Kempers
Associate Editor   Matthew W. Baker
Assistant Editor   Janet S. Parrack
Editorial Assistant   Cynthia C. Sawaya
Association Editor   David K. Roberts
Production Department Manager   Iona Sauscermen
Graphic Design Coordinator   Boni Nash
Design Consultant   Larry F. Husfelt
Electronic Publishing Supervisor   Wendy A. Mazur
Electronic Publishing Specialist   Anette Schütz-Ruff
Electronic Publishing Specialist   Cheryl J. Strum
Electronic Publishing Assistant   Peggy Mason

Cover Photo Credits   Cleo Freelance Photography

ISBN 0-87207-243-6

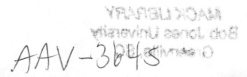

Contents

A few years ago while waiting in line at an airport newsstand, I spied an old friend. At least I *thought* it was an old friend. Indeed, I hadn't seen the friend in more than 40 years and therefore thought I might be mistaken. So I stepped out of line to get a better look. And the closer look proved it was the "old friend" I hadn't seen since I was seven years old.

To be more exact, the old friend was a copy of *The Babe Ruth Story*, the one my father had read to me each week when it was serialized in the pages of *The Saturday Evening Post* in February and March of 1948. Holding it in the airport I assumed the book had been reissued in conjunction with the release of actor John Goodman's film, *The Babe*.

One might ask, "How did I know for certain that *this* was the book my father had read to me?" I looked for the ghostwriter's name. You see, the Babe's power at the plate was not matched by his prowess at the tablet or typewriter, and thus he needed a ghostwriter to put his life into words. And each week, when my father hauled me atop his lap and turned to the next installment of the series, he would begin the reading with the same words: "*The Babe Ruth Story*, by Babe Ruth, *as told to* Bob Considine." And it was Considine's name I searched for that morning in the airport, the name that identified it as the exact one my father had read to me.

Why would someone remember the name of a ghostwriter of an article that had been read to him more than 40 years earlier? David Kherdian, the writer and poet, once explained it this way: "What we learn in childhood is carved in stone; what we learn in adulthood is carved in ice." The names of people I met last week or last night usually melt within hours or minutes. But what I learned as a child—the name of the street we tobogganed on, the man who owned the delicatessen, my grandmother's telephone number—those are carved in stone and last the ages.

Although both of my parents were literate people, neither ever attended college; indeed, my mother left school as a stenographer after tenth grade. Books and library cards were part of our home but not as much as magazines. There was just enough money for the necessities—the bus fare for Dad and the rent for our two-bedroom apartment in Union, New Jersey. For a long time, there was no car, no television; just three boys, then four, in a single bedroom. But somehow there was always enough money for magazines—perhaps because they were seen as necessities—maybe because they were (and still are) less expensive than books.

And it was magazines (and the daily newspaper) that made the biggest impact on my literacy, far more than any textbook in school. To begin with, I *saw* my parents reading magazines. Since the apple doesn't fall far from the tree, role modeling is very important here. When my father read to me, each reading was a lesson—though we didn't know it at the time.

He'd hold the cover of *The Post* in front of us and ask me what I thought the artist was trying to say. After we'd discussed it, he'd turn to the last page of the magazine and we'd read

"Hazel," the cartoon panel that years later would become the TV series with Shirley Booth. Humor is a very complicated thought process. In order to understand humor, one must be able to juggle two thoughts at the same time and simultaneously make a comparison of the two. You must picture in your mind: (1) the way things are in the joke; (2) the way things should be; and (3) compare the two in order to see the humorous contrast. That was the mental exercise my father and I went through with each "Hazel."

And then he would read me one of the stories from the magazine, explaining or paraphrasing (even editing out) what I didn't or shouldn't understand. The ideal thing would have been for him to share a children's magazine with me, but such entities were few and far between back in the 1940s. Today, as *Magazines for Kids and Teens* attests, there is no such shortage. The abundance of choices for magazines in all age groups requires a guide like this one to direct parents and educators through the plethora of publications.

Gradually something began to grow in our family. Because we saw our parents with magazines and because they'd been made available and appealing to us (through reading aloud), we became attracted to them. Their flexibility (as opposed to hard-bound books) and the brevity of their stories were also appealing. And I don't think the four Trelease brothers were any different from other teenagers when we made the "forbidden fruit" association with magazines; that is, since our teachers never assigned magazines to be read, we thought there was something verboten about them—thus they became even more attractive.

What we didn't know was that each night when we crawled into bed with our pile of magazines, we were going to school. Yes, my brother Brian's junior high English teachers might have been pulling their hair out over his unfinished worksheets, but what they didn't realize was that he was going to "night school"—lying in bed reading the likes of John Steinbeck, William Faulkner, and J.P. Marquand, whose works were being excerpted in the pages of *Sports Illustrated* in those days. He didn't know who those guys were; he just knew they were writing about sports and that's what he liked. (The greatest learning takes place at the point of interest.) And the more Brian read, the better he got at it, gradually moving out of the remedial group, through the D's, and eventually to college and a master's degree.

What many educators now have begun to realize is that reading is reading, whether you're using a textbook, a cookbook, a comic book, a newspaper, or a magazine. The only way to get better at it is by doing it. How do we get children to read more? By tying the act to their interests. With the variety now available in publishing and with guides like this one in your hand, that's the easy part—connecting a music fan, a gymnast, a computer whiz, or a Scout to the appropriate magazine.

Real literacy is more *caught* than *taught*. Most of the time we're unaware the *catching* is taking place. The same rules for grammar, spelling, and punctuation exist in magazines as in textbooks. The difference usually is that magazines you enjoy reading, textbooks you endure reading. But as the parade of words and sentences fly by your eyes and make minuscule connections throughout your brain, you are observing and absorbing how and when to use a certain word or punctuation. Call it "copy-cat learning."

Because reading is really the mental absorption of writing, we often end up writing the way we read. One example is Tony Hillerman, the popular adult mystery writer of the American southwest. Hillerman grew up in Oklahoma, a third-generation German American, and attended an American Indian boarding school for farm children. After receiving a journalism degree from the University of Oklahoma, he worked for years as a wire service reporter and then as an editor with *The Santa Fe New Mexican*. With that varied background, whom did he imitate when he became a novelist? Hillerman once wrote, "When my first book (*The Blessing Way*) was published, a reviewer said it was reminiscent of the Australian writer Arthur Upfield. I looked at that and said, 'Aw, yeah! I betcha.' So I went to the library and found some Upfield, and sure enough."

The Upfield connection had been established when Hillerman was a young boy, peddling *The Saturday Evening Post*—which often serialized the Australian's novels about an aborigine detective. Before delivering the copies, Hillerman would read (and absorb) each issue. In retrospect, Hillerman says, "I went through all my life with these incredible memories from that serial, of the Australian outback and the aboriginal culture. I just loved it."

I know just how Hillerman felt when he discovered the connection—kind of like finding an old friend in the newsstand at the airport. Those magazine connections are carved in stone and carved with pleasure.

If you are like most people, you probably picked up *Magazines for Kids and Teens* and flipped through it just like you would a magazine. Good! That's the way we designed it.

First, you probably looked for listings of familiar publications. Then you scanned the other listings, looking for a title that interested you, and maybe you discovered how the listings are arranged. Finally, you looked at the front of the book, and you found this page, which is provocatively titled with a big, bold "**How to....**" Researchers tell us these are the two strongest words in a magazine headline.

You follow this procedure because you are "magazine literate." You have learned how to quickly figure out how a publication works—how it's organized, where to find information, and how to gauge whether it fits into your life and interests. But magazine literacy also involves knowing how to get the most from a magazine.

Magazines for Kids and Teens provides a tool to help you, your students, your children or your teens, and anyone else for whom the reading habit is important, develop and refine magazine literacy. But first some background.

There are tens of thousands of magazines and periodicals published around the world, and all of them are unique in some way. Obviously, magazines vary in subject matter and approach, but even magazines that focus on the same subject and have the same reader profile differ from each other. Magazines reflect different personalities that make one magazine appealing and another very similar magazine not as appealing. Readers need to see whether or not they like different magazines by sampling many different types to see if they are a good "fit" with the reader.

Because many young readers have difficulty knowing what they like and most children's magazines and many teen magazines are not widely available on newsstands, finding the right fit can be tricky. The solution is to gather samples of magazines appropriate to the age and interests of the young reader and allow opportunities for browsing. Here are some suggestions for creating a browsing collection without breaking the bank:

- Search through the indexes at the end of *Magazines for Kids and Teens*. One lists magazines by age/grade, another by subject. Identify 15 to 20 magazines that might interest your young reader.
- Look up the magazine in *Magazines for Kids and Teens*. Read the listing and determine whether your selections are suitable and whether they are likely to be available locally for purchase.
- Note which magazines are favored in waiting rooms and in the homes of friends. Ask others with young readers of similar reading levels and interests which magazines are popular. Look up these in *Magazines for Kids and Teens* as well.

- If your choices are available on newsstands, purchase a copy. If not, scan the collections at local and school libraries. Encourage your young reader to look at a minimum of four or five magazines.
- Most magazines listed in this book indicate how to obtain a sample copy. Some publishers charge a fee, but many do not. Most are willing to incur the expense of sending samples to potential subscribers because they know this is an excellent way to generate those subscriptions.
- Create your own library from these samples. Give your young readers a month or two to pick which two, three, four or more magazines you should order. You can pass the unwanted magazines on to friends, relatives, librarians, and teachers.
- Order the magazines in your child's name. Few things bring bigger smiles to young readers than getting something addressed to them in the mail!
- When his or her subscription starts, work with your young reader to master the basics of magazine literacy such as using a table of contents and identifying the difference between editorial and advertising copy.

Reading and enjoying magazines can help your young reader develop a lifelong reading habit, one of life's most valuable assets.

How Children and Teens Can Publish Their Writing

Some young readers are not content to simply develop magazine literacy. They want to create the experiences that the writing of others has created for them; they want to write and have their writing published.

Editors and publishers of children's and teens' magazines recognize and value this impulse. Many offer a wide range of opportunities for young writers to have their work published. These opportunities range from publications that consist solely of young writers' work such as *Merlyn's Pen*, *New Moon*, and *Stone Soup*, to those publishing an occasional reader-generated article, story, poem, advice column, or editorial, to those publishing only readers' letters and drawings.

Although few publications pay for reader-created material, the thrill a young writer or artist feels when seeing his or her name in print is great indeed. *Magazines for Kids and Teens* can help the hopeful young contributor reach this goal. Here are some suggestions.

- Listings in *Magazines for Kids and Teens* include a notation entitled "Readers' Work Published." Those magazines that do accept readers' work are listed in a separate index.

- All potential young contributors must realize that magazines publish work that is of value to the magazine's readership. The secret is to submit good work within the magazine's guidelines.

- To determine whether work is likely to be accepted, look through your browsing copies to see what type of writing those magazines publish. To expand your sample library, follow the procedure outlined earlier.

- Editors will tell potential contributors that the best way to know what the magazine wants is to look at the content of the magazine. Are the letters, poems, and drawings tied to the theme of the issue? Are the letters long or short? What kinds of jokes do the editors think their readers will enjoy?

- Many magazines use writer's guidelines to tell potential contributors what they are looking for. These may be requested directly from the editor.

- Don't get discouraged. It is never the contributor who is rejected, it is the contribution. Each new piece of work is a new opportunity. Try other publications as well.

- Use *Magazines for Kids and Teens* to discover new outlets for contributions. Many of the publications accept contributors' work. Those with small circulations or with limited geographical distribution may not get as many contributions as larger, more established magazines, and these could be good magazines to try.

The excitement of sending a letter to the editor or sending a drawing to a magazine and the encouragement that comes with having that contribution published ranks with the best of all experiences young creators can have. Although most contributions are not used, and very few magazines return submissions or personally acknowledge all submissions whether they are used or not, some are published. Tailoring the submission to the publication makes a significant difference.

Acknowledgments

Thanks...

Magazines for Kids and Teens grew from the fertile mind of Kent Brown, editor of *Highlights for Children*, during his tenure as EdPress president. It was nurtured by Jennifer Stevenson, former director of publications at the International Reading Association and also a former president of EdPress. Nourishment continues to be provided by Joan Irwin, IRA director of publications, her talented staff, particularly Wendy Russ and Janet Parrack, and the EdPress staff, particularly Alana Peterson and David Dilks. And, my thanks to Jim Trelease for his inspiring foreword.

Julie Mercier, former managing director of EdPress, made the book happen. She found the new kids on the block, kept in contact with the establishment, chronicled the changes in ownership and personnel, and bid reluctant good-byes to those magazines who closed their doors since 1994. The original book design belongs to her.

As always, grateful thanks go to the EdPress executive board and to my family, Pat and Genevieve, who provided encouragement, help, support, and an occasional icepop.

Two other acknowledgments—one to the people behind the magazines that go to kids and teens—the editors, the writers, the art directors, the artists and illustrators, the marketing people, the researchers, the publishers, and everyone else who gives of themselves to make the magazines. Thank you for doing what you do.

The second acknowledgment goes to the parents, the teachers, the librarians, the reading specialists, the uncles, aunts, and grandparents—everyone who brings young readers to the wonders of these magazines. Keep up the good work and spread the word.

ABC (Barnabladid abc)

from Iceland, carries a wide selection of articles and stories. Accepts children's letters and uses reader input to shape editorial content.

Audience: M/F, ages 6–14
Subject: General interest and participation
Circulation: 10,000
Editor: Hildur Gisladottir
Publisher: Frødi, Ltd.

Editorial & Ordering Address:
Frødi, Ltd.
Armule 18
108 Reykjavik, Iceland
354-1-812300
Fax: 354-1-812946

Abrams Planetarium Sky Calendar

provides a night-by-night description of noteworthy sky events and includes a simplified star chart of the month's evening sky. The calendar, text, and sky chart are designed to be accessible for the beginning astronomer equipped with the naked eye and binoculars. Single 2-sided sheet for each month mailed quarterly.

Audience: M/F, ages 8–17
Subject: Astronomy (sky observing)
Circulation: 12,000 individual subscribers plus 4,000 bulk orders
Distribution: Homes, teachers, libraries, astronomy clubs, planetarium bookshops
Editor: Robert C. Victor
Publisher: Abrams Planetarium, Michigan State University
Cost: $7.50/yr.

Editorial & Ordering Address:
Sky Calendar
Abrams Planetarium
Michigan State University
East Lansing, MI 48824
517-355-4676

The Acorn

publishes children's work and aims to provide a showcase for young authors and those writing for K–12. It also seeks to be a teaching tool and informational guide to workshops and markets.

Audience: M/F, grades K–12
Subject: Fiction and poetry on any subject
Circulation: 100
Distribution: Schools (10%); other (90%)
Editor: Betty Chezum Mowery
Cost: $10.00 (4 issues)
Sample: $2.00
Readers' Work Published: Fiction, nonfiction, articles, poetry; send SASE for return of materials

Editorial & Ordering Address:
1530 Seventh Street
Rock Island, IL 61201
309-788-3980

Aerostato (Balloon)

Audience: M/F, ages 9–14
Subject: Greek culture
Circulation: 11,000
Editor: Anthoula Daniil–Ageliki Korkovelou
Publisher: Greek Ministry of Education
Cost: 300 drch/issue
Readers' Work Published: Yes

published in Greek, is for Greek children who live abroad. Its purpose is to keep them in touch with their country, language, manners, and customs. The subjects are news from Greece (festivals, shows, theater, etc.) and stories, tales, comics, Greek food, etc. This 64-page quarterly first appeared in April 1985.

Editorial & Ordering Address:
Greek Ministry of Education
15, Metropoleos Strasse
10185 Athens, Greece
01-3237336

Æskan (The Youth)

Audience: M/F, ages 7–14
Subject: General (stories, articles, puzzles, cartoons, jokes)
Circulation: 7,000
Editor: Karl Helgason
Publisher: The Icelandic Division of International Organization of Good Templars
Cost: $57.00/yr.
Sample: Write to editorial address
Readers' Work Published: Stories, drawings, pictures, letters

seeks to entertain children as well as develop their moral sense by reminding them of the advantage of a healthy life and total abstinence. The magazine attempts to stimulate the intellectual and creative abilities in youth and to preserve the Icelandic language.

Editorial & Ordering Address:
Eiridsgata 5
P.O. Box 523
121 Reykjavik, Iceland
354-1-10248
Fax: 354-1-10248

Ahora

Audience: M/F, ages 11–16
Subject: Spanish language, sports, TV, film, pop, teen culture, Spanish and Latin American culture
Circulation: 90,000
Distribution: Schools for classroom-home usage
Editor: Marta Giddings
Publisher: Mary Glasgow Magazines
Cost: $6.95/school yr.
Sample: Contact Scholastic Inc.
Readers' Work Published: Letters, artwork, photos

is in Spanish for teenagers learning Spanish at school. It covers topics of interest to the age group, at the same time introducing information and cultural details so that readers learn more about the language and background of the countries where Spanish is spoken. Its goal is to make Spanish come alive for its readers.

Editorial Address:
Mary Glasgow Magazines
Commonwealth House
1–19 New Oxford Street
London, England WC1A 1NU
441-71-4219050
Fax: 441-71-4219052

Ordering Address:
Scholastic Inc.
2931 East McCarty Street
P.O. Box 3710
Jefferson City, MO 65102-3710

AIM—America's Intercultural Magazine

is a quarterly featuring essays, short stories, and articles that promote racial harmony. Through the written word, the magazine seeks to point out how alike different cultures are.

Audience: M/F, high school, young adults, college
Subject: Materials of social significance
Distribution: Subscriptions
Editor: Ruth Apilado
Publisher: Ruth Apilado
Cost: $2.50/issue (4 issues/yr.)
Sample: $4.00
Readers' Work Published: Sometimes

Editorial Address:
7308 S. Eberhart Avenue
Chicago, IL 60619
312-874-6184

Ordering Address:
P.O. Box 20554
Chicago, IL 60620

Aktuell

is in German for teenagers learning German at school. It covers topics of interest to the age group, at the same time introducing information and cultural details so that readers learn more about the language and background of the countries where German is spoken. Its goal is to make German come alive for its readers.

Audience: M/F, ages 11–16
Subject: German language, sports, TV, film, pop, teen culture
Distribution: Schools, homes
Editor: Miroslav Imbresevic
Publisher: Mary Glasgow Magazines
Cost: $6.95 (6 issues)
Sample: Free from ordering address

Editorial Address:
Mary Glasgow Magazines
Commonwealth House
1–19 New Oxford Street
London, England WC1A 1NU
441-71-4219050
Fax: 441-71-4219052

Ordering Address:
Scholastic Inc.
2931 East McCarty Street
P.O. Box 3710
Jefferson City, MO 65102-3710

Alateen Talk

is the teen newsletter of the Al-Anon family group, featuring letters and artwork from the international Alateen membership (younger family members affected by someone else's drinking) sharing experiences, strengths, and hopes. Their stories relate their personal lives, how their Alateen group is functioning, and ways in which to carry the Alateen message to younger people who are still suffering from someone else's drinking.

Audience: M/F, ages 7–17
Subject: Variety of topics
Circulation: 10,000
Distribution: All registered groups and subscribers
Editor: Alateen Administrator
Publisher: Al-Anon Family Groups
Cost: $2.50/subscription (10 issues); $7.50 for 10 sets
Readers' Work Published: Sharings from children affected by someone's drinking

Editorial & Ordering Address:
Al-Anon Family Group Headquarters, Inc.
1600 Corporate Landing Parkway
Virginia Beach, VA 23454
757-563-1600

Allons-y!

is in French for teenagers learning French at school. It covers topics of interest to the age group, at the same time introducing information and cultural details so that readers learn more about the language and background of the countries where French is spoken. Its goal is to make French come alive for its readers.

Audience: M/F, ages 11–16
Subject: French language, sports, TV, film, pop, teen culture, French and Francophone culture
Circulation: 70,000
Distribution: Schools for classroom-home usage
Editor: Halim Benzine
Publisher: Mary Glasgow Magazines
Cost: $6.95/school yr.
Sample: Contact Scholastic Inc.
Readers' Work Published: Letters, artwork, photos

Editorial Address:
Mary Glasgow Magazines
Commonwealth House
1–19 New Oxford Street
London, England WC1A 1NU
441-71-4219050
Fax: 441-71-4219052

Ordering Address:
Scholastic Inc.
2931 East McCarty Street
P.O. Box 3710
Jefferson City, MO 65102-3710

American Careers

profiles career fields, examines labor trends, presents statistics, and discusses issues related to career decisions for junior high students. Colorful and engaging articles by experts are complemented by student-written work. *American Careers* seeks to use a challenging, critical thinking approach to career awareness, education options, and personal growth. Each issue is accompanied by a teaching guide.

Audience: M/F, ages 12–16
Subject: Career awareness and related issues
Circulation: 500,000+
Distribution: Classrooms (100%)
Editor: Barbara F. Orwig
Publisher: Career Communications, Inc.
Cost: $7.50/yr. (3 issues); $22.50/classroom set (25 copies)
Sample: On written request
Readers' Work Published: Unsolicited cartoons, articles, puzzles—all submissions acknowledged —no compensation to authors or creators

Editorial & Ordering Address:
Career Communications, Inc.
6701 W. 64th Street
Suite 304
Overland Park, KS 66202
913-362-7788

American Craft

celebrates the importance of handicrafts by reporting on outstanding work being done in clay, fiber, metal, glass, wood, and other media. Features include profiles of master craftsmen, exhibition and book reviews, a "Gallery" of exhibited works, a news section, and a national calendar of craft events.

Audience: M/F, high school (ages 14–18)
Subject: Contemporary American crafts
Circulation: 45,000
Editor: Lois Moran
Publisher: Lois Moran
Cost: $5.00/issue; $40.00/yr. (6 issues)
Sample: On written request

Editorial & Ordering Address:
American Craft Council
72 Spring Street
New York, NY 10012
212-274-0630

American Girl

celebrates girlhood yesterday and today. It reflects a sense that girls should not be pushed to grow up too soon. Articles, fiction, and features focus on the accomplishments and interests of girls in an engaging and colorful fashion. The magazine includes letters and an array of activities. Characters from the American Girls Collection are featured.

Audience: F, ages 8 and up
Subject: General interest
Circulation: 650,000
Distribution: Newsstands, subscriptions
Editor: Judith Woodburn
Publisher: Pleasant T. Rowland, Pleasant Company Publications, Inc.
Cost: $3.95/issue; $19.95/yr. (6 issues)
Sample: Send $3.95 along with SASE w/$1.93 in U.S. postage to the Magazine Dept. Asst.
Readers' Work Published: Letters, comments, jokes, anecdotes, poems

Editorial Address:
Pleasant Company
   Publications, Inc.
8400 Fairway Place
Middleton, WI 53562-0986
608-836-4848
Fax: 608-831-7089
E-mail: ageditor@ag.pleasantco.com

Ordering Address:
Pleasant Company
   Publications, Inc.
8400 Fairway Place
P.O. Box 62986
Middleton, WI 53562-0986
800-234-1278

Animals

is the nation's leading magazine for animal enthusiasts and the only magazine that combines coverage of pets and pet care with wildlife, environmental, and animal-protection concerns. Each issue is dedicated to entertaining and informing readers with balanced, award-winning journalism and spectacular photography of domestic and wild animals—and the people who share their habitats—around the world. Founded in 1868, *Animals* is published by the Massachusetts Society for the Prevention of Cruelty to Animals and the American Humane Education Society.

Audience: M/F, young adult, adult
Subject: Pets, wildlife, animal protection
Circulation: 95,000
Distribution: Newsstands, subscriptions, online
Editor: Joni Praded
Publisher: MSPCA/AHES
Cost: $19.94/yr.

Editorial Address:
MSPCA/AHES
350 South Huntington Avenue
Boston, MA 02130
617-541-5065
Fax: 617-522-4885

Ordering Address:
Animals Subscription Services
P.O. Box 581
Mt. Morris, IL 61054
800-998-0797

Astrapi

Audience: M/F, ages 7–10
Subject: General interest (sciences, nature, history)
Circulation: 79,996
Distribution: Homes, newsstands, schools
Editor: Catherine Peugeot
Publisher: Bayard Presse
Cost: 28 FF/issue; 559 FF/yr.

is a general interest magazine, rich and varied, and full of interactive features and humor, for children ages 7–10. It's really three magazines in one, with a little encyclopedia that takes a different form every month, tackling many subjects; a magazine with photographic wildlife reports, parent and children's supplements, games and crafts, and cartoons; and a little journal with a news section that explains to children what's going on around them.

Editorial Address:
Bayard Presse
3 rue Bayard
Paris 75008, France
331-44-356060
Fax: 331-44-35604

Ordering Address:
Bayard Presse International
BP 12
99505 Paris Entreprise France
331-44-216000
Fax: 331-20-274192

AutoWeek

Audience: M/F, young adult, adult
Subject: New cars, racing
Circulation: 275,000
Distribution: Homes (95%); newsstands (5%)
Editor: Matt DeLorenzo
Publisher: Leon Mandel
Cost: $28.00/yr.

publishes the latest information on cars—new and classic—motorshows, the major racing series, Indy cars, stockers, and F-1 for the automotive enthusiast.

Editorial Address:
Crain Communications
1400 Woodbridge Avenue
Detroit, MI 48207
313-446-6000
Fax: 313-446-0347

Ordering Address:
Autoweek Circulation
965 E. Jefferson Avenue
Detroit, MI 48207
313-446-0486

Babar

Audience: M/F, ages 3–7
Subject: Babar's stories, games
Circulation: 54,355
Distribution: subscriptions, schools, newsstands
Editor: Pascale Chenel
Publisher: Bayard Presse
Cost: 20 FF/issue; 199 FF/yr.

is a classic for all children. Every month young readers rediscover the fantastic and reassuring world of the famous Babar, made very popular by the television series. Around the character of Babar, his wife Celeste, their children Pom, Flore, Alexander, and the other characters in his world, there are stories, a notebook, color prints ("Babarama"), features about the animal kingdom, and children's cartoons.

Editorial Address:
Bayard Presse
3 rue Bayard
Paris 75008, France
331-44-356060
Fax: 331-44-35604

Ordering Address:
Bayard Presse International
BP 12
99505 Paris Entreprise France
331-44-216000

Babybug

is a board-book magazine that is designed for small hands. It's made of sturdy cardboard pages (6 1/4 × 7 inches) with rounded corners and no staples. It is filled with simple stories, rhymes, and colorful pictures that babies and parents will enjoy together again and again.

Audience: M/F, ages 6 months–2 yrs.
Subject: Stories, rhymes, pictures
Circulation: 44,000
Editor: Marianne Carus, Editor-in-Chief
Publisher: Robert W. Harper
Cost: $5.00/issue; $32.97/yr. (12 issues)
Sample: Send $5.00 to Mary Beth Maklavcic at editorial address

Editorial Address:
Babybug
315 Fifth Street
Peru, IL 61354
815-224-6656

Ordering Address:
Babybug
P.O. Box 7436
Red Oak, IA 51591-4436
800-827-0227

Balls & Strikes

highlights the activities of the adults and children who play softball through the ASA's 101 state/metro associations. *B&S* has monthly features on players and events, news on trends and major headlines in the sport, reports on new products, and tournament schedules and results.

Audience: M/F, ages 18 and under
Subject: Softball
Circulation: 300,000
Distribution: Homes (100%)
Editor: Ronald A. Babb
Publisher: Donald E. Porter
Cost: $2.00/issue; $16.00/yr. (8 issues)
Sample: Write Ronald A. Babb or Bill Plummer III at address provided
Readers' Work Published: Yes

Editorial & Ordering Address:
Amateur Softball Association
2801 N.E. 50th Street
Oklahoma City, OK 73111
405-424-5266
Fax: 405-424-3855

Barbie, The Magazine for Girls

is a fashion/lifestyle magazine for girls ages 5–12, focusing on the latest trends in fashion, entertainment, and the world of Barbie. Its goal is to entertain little girls and help them realize their potential. It relies heavily on readers' letters and comments to devise editorial content.

Audience: F, ages 5–12
Subject: Fashion, entertainment, the world of Barbie
Circulation: 600,000
Distribution: Newsstands, subscriptions
Editor: Polly Chevalier
Publisher: Donald E. Welsh, Welsh Publishing Group
Cost: $1.95/issue; $12.25/yr. (6 issues)
Readers' Work Published: Letters, art, photos of readers with their Barbie collections

Editorial Address:
Marvel Entertainment
    Group, Inc.
387 Park Avenue
New York, NY 10016
212-576-4042
Fax: 212-576-9289

Ordering Address:
P.O. Box 10798
Des Moines, IA 50340
515-243-4543

Beijing Review

is an English-language weekly carrying news and views from China. It provides information on government policies; progress and problems of the Chinese people in their political, economic, cultural, and social development; philosophy, theories, and principles of the Chinese communist party; Chinese stands and views on major international issues; and the changing lives of China's 56 ethnic nationalities.

Audience: M/F, young adults, adults
Subject: Policies, new developments, population, education in China
Circulation: 10,000 in U.S.; 120,000 worldwide
Distribution: Individual subscriptions, libraries
Editor: Shang Rongguang, North American Rep.
Publisher: Beijing Review
Cost: $35.80/yr. (51 issues)
Readers' Work Published: Letters

Editorial Address:
24 Baiwanzhuang Road
Beijing, 100037
China
861-831-4318

Ordering Address:
Mr. Geng Yuxin,
China Books and
 Periodicals, Inc.
2929 24th Street
San Francisco, CA 94110
415-282-2992
Fax: 415-282-0992

Black Belt for Kids

promotes the positive aspects of martial arts training and features inspirational stories involving martial arts role models. The magazine avoids excessive violence and aggression often associated with martial arts.

Audience: M/F, ages 5–16
Subject: Martial arts celebrities, TV shows, safety, educational
Circulation: 35,000
Editor: Robert W. Young
Publisher: Michael James
Cost: $2.95/issue; $9.75/yr.
Sample: Free with 9" × 12" SASE
Readers' Work Published: Letters, 1st person accounts, art

Editorial & Ordering Address:
Rainbow Publications
P.O. Box 918
Santa Clarita, CA 91380
805-257-4066

The Black Collegian

provides black college students with the information they need to succeed in college and in the workplace. Information on who is hiring, who the committed equal opportunity employers are, and how to prepare for a job search can be found in most issues. Information on fellowships, scholarships, internships, and study abroad is also given.

Audience: M/F, young adults
Subject: Educational/career opportunities and information
Circulation: 112,322
Distribution: Students (98.2%); college faculty (.1%); libraries/education centers (1.7%)
Publisher: Preston Edwards
Cost: $4.00/yr. (students); $8.00/yr. (regular)
Sample: Call or write circulation manager

Editorial Address:
The Black Collegian
140 Carondelet Street
New Orleans, LA 70130
504-523-0154
Fax: 504-523-0271

Ordering Address:
Black Collegiate Services
Nina Reese,
 Circulation Manager
140 Carondelet Street
New Orleans, LA 70130
504-523-0154
Fax: 504-523-0271

Blue Jean Magazine

Audience: F, ages 13–19
Subject: Career profiles, daring teen feats, community challenges, environment reporting
Circulation: 100,000+
Editor: Sherry S. Handel
Cost: $5.95/issue; $29.00/yr. (6 issues)
Sample: $8.00
Readers' Work Published: Fiction, nonfiction, poetry, artwork, photography (send SASE for submission guidelines)

portrays real teen girls on the verge of changing the world. The magazine is multicultural and advertisement free, devoted to publishing what teen girls are thinking, saying, and doing. No dieting or make-up tips—or super models. *Blue Jean* accepts artwork, poetry, photography, and fiction and nonfiction works from girls across the United States. Authors/artists are compensated for work published. Send SASE for submission guidelines.

Editorial & Ordering Address:
Blue Jean Magazine
P.O. Box 90856
Rochester, NY 14609
716-654-5070
Fax: 716-654-6785
E-mail: bluejeanmg@aol.com

Bonjour

Audience: M/F, ages 13–15
Subject: French language, general interest
Circulation: 70,000
Distribution: Schools
Editor: Halim Benzine
Publisher: Mary Glasgow Magazines
Cost: $6.95/subscription (6 issues)
Sample: Free on request to Scholastic Inc.

is written in French for teenagers learning French at school. It covers topics of interest to the age group, at the same time introducing information and cultural details so that readers learn the language and background of the countries where French is spoken. Its goal is to make French come alive for its readers.

Editorial Address:
Mary Glasgow Magazines
Commonwealth House
1–19 New Oxford Street
London, England WC1A 1NU
441-71-4219050
Fax: 441-71-4219052

Ordering Address:
Scholastic Inc.
2931 East McCarty Street
P.O. Box 3710
Jefferson City, MO 65102-3710

Boodle

Audience: M/F, ages 6–13
Subject: Stories, poems, artwork by kids
Circulation: 1,500
Distribution: Schools (60%); homes (40%)
Editor: Mavis Catalfio
Publisher: Jack Ronald
Cost: $3.00/issue; $10.00/yr. (4 quarterly issues)
Sample: $2.50
Readers' Work Published: Stories, poems, puzzles, artwork

is a "by-kids-for-kids" magazine featuring upbeat, fun stories, puzzles, artwork, and poetry by kids 6- to 13-years old. The goal is for readers to say "I can do that!" and begin their own writing and creative work.

Editorial & Ordering Address:
Graphic Printing Co.
P.O. Box 1049
Portland, IN 47371
219-726-8141
Fax: 219-726-8143

Audience: M/F, ages 6–12
Subject: General interest
Circulation: 34,000
Distribution: Homes (80%); school libraries (10%); newsstands, retail (5%)
Editor: David Strom
Publisher: Listen and Learn Home Education, Inc.
Cost: $7.95/issue; $39.95/yr. (12 issues) plus $4.00 postage and handling
Sample: Call toll-free number or send $3.00 postage to ordering address
Readers' Work Published: Letters, interviews, audio clips

Boomerang! The Children's Audio Magazine About Big Ideas

a monthly children's audio magazine, is designed to entertain and inform children 6- to 12-years old. Presented in children's voices and in story form, each cassette issue features segments on current events, economics, history, geography, music, mysteries, jokes, and more. All accompanied by a 7-fold insert featuring games, fun facts, and recommended reading.

Editorial & Ordering Address:
Box 261
La Honda, CA 94020
800-333-7858
415-747-0978
Fax: 800-333-7858

Audience: M, ages 7–18
Subject: General interest
Circulation: 1,300,000
Distribution: Homes
Editor: J.D. Owen
Publisher: J. Warren Young
Cost: $2.60/issue; $15.60/yr. (12 issues)
Sample: Contact Margie Bolton at ordering address; send 9" × 12" SASE and $2.50 per issue

Boys' Life

is a general interest, 4-color monthly, published by the Boy Scouts of America since 1911. Known as "The Magazine for All Boys," its mission is to entertain and educate America's youth and to open their eyes to the joyous world of reading. It features a proven mix of news, nature, sports, history, fiction, science, comics, and Scouting. Lively writing enhances a wide range of story topics illustrated with colorful graphics and photos. The magazine offers variety and substance, is written simply (but not downward), and carefully measures reader response through surveys.

Editorial Address:
Boy Scouts of America
1325 Walnut Hill Lane
P.O. Box 152079
Irving, TX 75015-2079
214-580-2366

Ordering Address:
Subscription Service
1325 Walnut Hill Lane
P.O. Box 152079
Irving, TX 75015-2079
214-580-2512

Bread for God's Children

is designed as a teaching tool for Christian families, with a monthly Bible study and articles to help bring an understanding of God's Word and practical applications to daily living.

Audience: M/F, children and adults
Subject: A teaching magazine for Christian families
Circulation: 10,000 U.S. and Canada
Distribution: Homes (90%); churches (5%); other— schools, prisons, libraries (5%)
Editor: Judith Gibbs
Cost: Free—supported through offerings
Sample: Sent on request
Readers' Work Published: One page of children's letters, stories and poems

Editorial & Ordering Address:
Bread Ministries
P.O. Box 1017
Arcadia, FL 34265-1017
941-494-6214
Fax: 941-993-0154

Brilliant Star

is an international magazine that seeks to serve the needs of English-speaking Baha'i children of all ages by confirming their Baha'i identity and helping them to become Baha'i teachers.

Audience: M/F, grades 1–6
Subject: Baha'i faith
Circulation: 1,800
Distribution: Subscriptions, bulk orders
Editor: Pepper Peterson Oldziey
Publisher: National Spiritual Assembly of the Baha'is of the United States
Cost: $3.50/issue; $18.00/yr. (6 issues)
Sample: Send SASE with U.S. postage for 6 oz.
Readers' Work Published: Any kind that fits the theme

Editorial Address:
Baha'i National Center
Wilmette, IL 60091
302-734-3684
Fax: 302-736-5034
E-mail: bstar@usbnc.org
Orders: 847-251-1854, ext. 11

ByLine

is a U.S. national magazine seeking to help all writers, including young writers, succeed. *ByLine* carries a 2-page student feature each month from September through June presenting writing contests for students and printing the winning entries. Tips concerning how to construct winning entries are included, and winners receive a cash prize. A small entry fee (usually $1) is required.

Audience: M/F, adults with student page
Subject: Writing and writing techniques
Circulation: 3,000
Distribution: Mail and at writers' conferences
Editor: Marcia Preston
Publisher: Marcia Preston
Cost: $20.00/yr. (11 issues)
Sample: $4.00
Readers' Work Published: Winners of our student writing contests only

Editorial & Ordering Address:
P.O. Box 130596
Edmond, OK 73013-0001
405-348-5591
E-mail: bylinemp@aol.com

Audience: M/F, ages 11–16
Subject: French language, general interest
Distribution: Schools
Editor: Halim Benzine
Publisher: Mary Glasgow Magazines
Cost: $6.95/subscription (6 issues)
Sample: Available from ordering address

Ca Va?

is written in French for teenagers learning French at school. It covers topics of interest to the age group, at the same time introducing information and cultural details so that readers learn the language and background of the countries where French is spoken. Its goal is to make French come alive for its readers.

Editorial Address:
Mary Glasgow Magazines
Commonwealth House
1–19 New Oxford Street
London, England WC1A 1NU
441-71-4219050
Fax: 441-71-4219052

Ordering Address:
Scholastic Inc.
2931 East McCarty Street
P.O. Box 3710
Jefferson City, MO 65102-3710

Audience: M/F, ages 9–11 and up
Subject: California history and geography
Circulation: 20,000
Distribution: Schools and some libraries
Editor: Rice Oliver
Publisher: Rice Oliver
Cost: $23.00/copy each of 34 issues with teacher guide; class sets at reduced rate
Sample: Call or fax request or mail on institution letterhead
Readers' Work Published: Area reports, geography, history

California Weekly Explorer

is designed for use in California's 4th grades. It seeks to excite students about their state's heritage and to stimulate the use of maps and biographies. Students are encouraged to use local resources to research and write local history. All 34 weekly issues are sent in advance so teachers may select which topics they wish to pursue.

Editorial & Ordering Address:
285 E. Main Street
Suite 3
Tustin, CA 92780
714-730-5991
Fax: 714-730-3548
E-mail: cwex@aol.com

Audience: M/F, ages 8–15
Subject: World history
Circulation: 8,000
Distribution: Schools and homes
Editor: Rosalie Baker
Publisher: Lyell C. Dawes, Cobblestone Publishing, Inc.
Cost: $18.95/yr. (5 issues)
Sample: Mail check for $5.70 with request to Cobblestone Publishing
Readers' Work Published: Letters

Calliope

is a 48-page, theme-related magazine. Its goal is to awaken in young people an interest in and deep appreciation for people and events of the past. Full-length articles, stories, time lines, maps, and historical photos make up every issue, which also includes departments on word origins, archaeology, and the importance of the past today.

Editorial & Ordering Address:
Cobblestone Publishing, Inc.
7 School Street
Peterborough, NH 03458
603-924-7209
Fax: 603-924-7380

Campus Life

is a magazine that seeks to help teenagers understand how Christian faith fits into all areas of their lives. With an emphasis on "the balanced life," *Campus Life* offers readers plenty of humor, true-experience stories from fellow teens, and advice pertinent to their everyday questions and concerns.

Audience: M/F, high school students
Subject: Concerns of high school students; editorial perspective/slant distinctively Christian
Circulation: 120,000
Distribution: Individual subscribers
Editor: Chris Lutes
Publisher: Christianity Today, Inc.
Cost: $2.00/issue; $14.95/yr.; $23.90/2 yrs.
Sample: Send $2.00 and SASE (9" × 12")
Readers' Work Published: "As-told-to" first-person stories, fiction

Editorial Address:
Christianity Today
465 Gundersen Drive
Carol Stream, IL 60188
708-260-6200
Fax: 708-260-0114

Ordering Address:
Campus Life/CTI
P.O. Box 11618
Des Moines, IA 50340-1618
800-678-6083

Canada and the World

is a current events magazine designed as a classroom teaching aid. Its aim is to help young people understand the complex issues that shape the world around them.

Audience: M/F, grades 9–12
Subject: Current events
Circulation: 18,000
Editor: Rupert J. Taylor
Publisher: R/L Taylor Consultants Publishing Limited
Cost: $2.50/issue; $22.00/yr. (9 issues)
Sample: Free; write to editorial address

Editorial & Ordering Address:
R/L Taylor Consultants Publishing
P.O. Box 7004
Oakville, ON
Canada L6J 6L5
416-338-3394

Canoe Magazine

provides full coverage of the sports canoeing and kayaking, including where-to-go, what-to-take, and how-to-use-it information. Family canoe/kayak camping, day tripping, whitewater, ocean, and competition all are featured.

Audience: M/F, all ages
Subject: Canoeing/kayaking
Circulation: 68,000
Distribution: Subscriptions (45%); newsstands (45%); outdoor specialty stores (10%)
Editor: David Harrison
Publisher: Judy C. Harrison
Cost: $17.95/yr. (6 issues)
Sample: Call 1-800-MYCA-NOE and request a sample copy

Editorial & Ordering Address:
Canoe America Associates
10526 N.E. 68th, Suite 3
P.O. Box 3146
Kirkland, WA 98083
206-827-6303
Fax: 206-827-1893

Career World

focuses on what a student needs to know about career planning in the world of work. Features include in-depth articles focusing on specific careers, jobs for students, and interviews with people in different careers.

Audience: M/F, ages 13–18
Subject: Career and vocational education
Circulation: 78,394
Distribution: Schools
Editor: Carole Rubenstein
Publisher: Richard J. LeBrasseur, Weekly Reader Corp.
Cost: $8.75/subscription for 15 or more sets (7 issues)

Editorial Address:
GLC
900 Skokie Boulevard
Northbrook, IL 60062-4028
847-205-3000
Fax: 847-564-8197
E-mail: glcprep@aol.com

Ordering Address:
Weekly Reader Corp.
3001 Cindel Drive
Delran, NJ 08370
800-446-3355

Careers & Colleges

seeks to promote the notion that young people have the power—and the responsibility—to shape their own futures. It provides readers with materials on career choices, life values, higher education, and other topics that will help prepare them for enjoyable and profitable work that will generate self-respect.

Audience: M/F, grades 11–12
Subject: Higher education, career options, and life beyond high school
Circulation: 500,000
Distribution: 2,000 U.S. high schools
Editor: June Rogoznica
Publisher: June Rogoznica
Cost: $2.50/issue; $5.00/yr. (2 issues)
Sample: Send SASE ($1.21 U.S. postage on 9" × 12" envelope) plus $2.50

Editorial & Ordering Address:
E.M. Guild, Inc.
99 Avenue of the Americas
New York, NY 10018
212-563-4688
Fax: 212-967-2531

Casper the Friendly Ghost

seeks to entertain children and help them understand the importance of friendship in their lives. It seeks to encourage readers to judge people only by individual behavior and never by background or appearance.

Audience: M/F, ages 5–9
Subject: Comics magazine
Circulation: 75,000
Distribution: Newsstands (90%); subscriptions (5%); direct market comics stores (5%)
Editor: Sidney Jacobson
Publisher: Jeffrey A. Montgomery, Harvey Comics Entertainment Company
Cost: $1.25/issue (12 issues)
Sample: Write to Kevin Bricklin, Publishing Director
Readers' Work Published: Letters, artwork

Editorial & Ordering Address:
Harvey Entertainment Company
100 Wilshire Boulevard
Suite 1400
Santa Monica, CA 90401-1110
310-451-3377
Fax: 310-458-6995

Cavall Fort

Audience: M/F, ages 10–14
Subject: Catalan language
and culture
Circulation: 20,000
Distribution: Homes (90%);
schools (5%); other (5%)
Editor: Albert Jané
Publisher: Revista per a Nois i
Noies Cavall Fort S.L.
Cost: 6.350 pta/yr.
Sample: A. Jané, Cavall Fort,
Lesseps 33,
08023 Barcelona, Spain
Readers' Work Published:
Two pages each issue

is a children's magazine in the Catalan language published since 1961. It appears twice a month and contains some of the best European comic series, comics' own productions, as well as tales, short stories, entertainment, pastimes, and cultural, scientific, historical, and literary information.

Editorial & Ordering Address:
Revista per a Nois i Noies Cavall Fort S.L.
Placa Lesseps, 33
08023 Barcelona, Spain
34-3-218-6220
Fax: 34-3-217-6100

Challenge

Audience: M, grades 7–12
Subject: Mission, teen issues,
effective Christian lifestyles
Circulation: 24,000
Distribution: Homes(5%);
churches (95%)
Editor: Jene C. Smith,
Challengers Materials
Publisher: Brotherhood
Commission, SBC
Cost: $3.09/quarter (monthly); $3.75/quarter, Leader
Edition
Sample: Send 9" × 12" SASE
plus 78¢ postage

is for young men, ages 12–18, grades 7–12, who are members of a missions organization in Southern Baptist churches. Articles are about interests and issues of teenagers, especially features on sports figures or artists who offer good, moral guidelines and effective Christian testimony.

Editorial Address:
Brotherhood Commission, SBC
1548 Poplar Avenue
Memphis, TN 38104
901-272-2461

Ordering Address:
Customer Services
Brotherhood Commission, SBC
1548 Poplar Ave.
Memphis, TN 38104
901-272-2461

Champs-Elyseés

Audience: M/F, high school
intermediate and advanced
French students
Subject: French language and
culture
Editor: Terry Lacassin
Publisher: Wes Green,
Champs-Elyseés, Inc.
Cost: $129.00/yr.; $79.00/
5 months
Sample: $20.00

produced in Paris, is a monthly magazine on audiocassette designed for intermediate and advanced students of French. It features interviews, music, and conversation about French news, politics, sports, art, books, restaurants, movies, and travel. Each cassette comes with a word-for-word printed transcript that includes an extensive French-English glossary.

Editorial & Ordering Address:
P.O. Box 158067
Nashville, TN 37215-8067
800-824-0829
Fax: 615-297-3138

Chem Matters Magazine

seeks to make chemistry accessible to high school students by expanding the chemistry classroom into the world surrounding it. It does so by describing real-life situations in terms of the chemistry involved in a series of feature articles, interviews, and photo essays.

Audience: M/F, high school students
Subject: Real-world application of chemistry
Circulation: 60,000
Editor: David P. Robson
Publisher: American Chemical Society
Cost: $2.50 (4 issues)

Editorial Address:
Towson State University
Department of Chemistry
Towson, MD 21204-7097
301-830-2635
Fax: 301-830-3394

Ordering Address:
American Chemical Society
1155 16th Street NW
Washington, DC 20036

Chess Life

seeks to promote the game of chess as an art form, as a game, as a sport, and as a useful classroom tool. It highlights the achievements of young United States Chess Federation members in the national elementary, junior high, and high school championships, All-American team, and the Tournament of High School Champions. Various instructional articles are regular features.

Audience: M/F, junior and senior high school
Subject: Chess
Circulation: 70,000
Distribution: Subscriptions (94%); newsstands (3%); libraries, clubs, classrooms (3%)
Editor: Glenn Petersen
Publisher: Al Lawrence, U.S. Chess Federation
Cost: $3.75/issue; $38.00/yr. (12 issues)
Sample: $1.00; write to U.S. Chess Federation
Readers' Work Published: Tournament reports

Editorial & Ordering Address:
United States Chess Federation
186 Route 9W
New Windsor, NY 12553
914-562-8350
Fax: 914-236-4852
E-mail: http://www.uschess.org

Chez Nous

is written in French for teenagers learning French at school. It covers topics of interest to the age group, at the same time introducing information and cultural details so that readers learn about the language and background of the countries where French is spoken. Its goal is to make French come alive for its readers.

Audience: M/F, ages 16–18
Subject: French language, general interest
Distribution: Schools
Editor: Halim Benzine
Publisher: Mary Glasgow Magazines
Cost: $6.95/subscription (6 issues)
Sample: Available from ordering address

Editorial Address:
Mary Glasgow Magazines
Commonwealth House
1–19 New Oxford Street
London, England WC1A 1NU
441-71-4219050
Fax: 441-71-4219052

Ordering Address:
Scholastic Inc.
2931 East McCarty Street
P.O. Box 3710
Jefferson City, MO 65102-3710

Chickadee Magazine

is a "hands-on" publication designed to introduce the world of science, nature and technology to children ages 8 and under. Each 32-page issue includes an easy-to-read animal story, a fiction story or poem, fun puzzles and games, a pull-out poster, a simple science experiment and contains color photos, illustrations, and drawings submitted by the readers.

Audience: M/F, ages 8 and under
Subject: Science, nature, animals, and technology
Circulation: 125,000 in Canada and U.S.
Distribution: Subscriptions (98%); other (2%)
Editor: Nyla Ahmad
Publisher: Owl Communications
Cost: $2.95/issue; $17.95/yr. U.S.
Sample: Available from ordering address

Editorial Address:
Owl Communications Inc.
179 John Street, Suite 500
Toronto, ON
Canada M5T 3G5
416-971-5275
Fax: 416-971-5294
E-mail: owlcom@owl.on.ca

Ordering Address:
In the U.S.
Chickadee Magazine
25 Boxwood Lane
Buffalo, NY 14227-2780

Child Life

is a general interest magazine with an emphasis on health. It attempts to introduce children to different cultures, personalities, mysteries of nature, and the creative ideas of other kids. *Child Life* also introduces readers to healthy living habits with articles on exercise, nutrition, and a question/answer column.

Audience: M/F, ages 9–11
Subject: General interest with health/fitness
Circulation: 65,000
Distribution: Subscriptions
Editor: Lise Hoffman
Publisher: Children's Better Health Institute
Cost: $16.95/yr. (8 issues)
Sample: $1.25 (includes postage)
Readers' Work Published: Stories, poems, jokes, photos, drawings

Editorial Address:
Children's Better Health Institute
1100 Waterway Boulevard
P.O. Box 567
Indianapolis, IN 46206
317-636-8881
Fax: 317-684-8094

Ordering Address:
P.O. Box 7133
Red Oak, IA 51591-0133
317-636-8881, ext. 233

Children's Digest

first published in 1950, features contemporary fiction—adventure, mysteries, science fiction, and stories—that realistically portray problems that preteens face today. Nonfiction takes a lively, informal approach to health issues. Regular columns cover food and nutrition, and the environment. *Children's Digest* encourages preteens to read and think.

Audience: M/F, preteen
Subject: General interest (esp. fitness and sports)
Circulation: 110,000
Distribution: Subscriptions
Editor: Layne Cameron
Publisher: Children's Better Health Institute
Cost: $13.95/yr. (8 issues)
Sample: $1.25 to the editorial address
Readers' Work Published: Original stories (not over 200 words), jokes, poems (no compensation; material cannot be returned)

Editorial & Ordering Address:
Children's Better Health Institute
1100 Waterway Boulevard
P.O. Box 567
Indianapolis, IN 46206
317-636-8881

Children's Magazine

published in Chinese, seeks to stimulate the intellectual and creative abilities in elementary school children ages 6–12. Based on the belief of a broad-minded human life, *Children's Magazine* attempts to encourage contemplation through literature, art, math, science, music, and daily life stories. This 104-page, 4-color, monthly magazine first appeared in October 1986.

Audience: M/F, ages 6–12
Subject: General interest
Circulation: 50,000
Distribution: Schools (96%); homes (3%); newsstands (1%)
Editor: Ho Chen-Kuang
Publisher: CHEN Yin-How, Director of Taiwan Provincial Dept. of Educ.
Cost: 130 NT/issue; 1300NT/yr.
Sample: Contact editor
Readers' Work Published: Compositions, stories, drawings created by children

Editorial Address:
Children's Book Publishing
5F, 172, Chung-Hsiao E. Road, Section 1
Taipei, Taiwan
Republic of China
886-2-3446194
Fax: 886-2-3416625

Ordering Address:
Taiwan Book Store
18, Chung-Ching S. Road, Section 1
Taipei, Taiwan
Republic of China
886-2-3820222/3820232

Children's Playmate

features stories, poems, activities, recipes, and crafts for children ages 6–8. The magazine encourages good health habits and wholesome values. The focus is to entertain and inform, so that children are better able to make healthy choices. The goal is to ignite a passion for reading that will last a lifetime.

Audience: M/F, ages 6–8
Subject: Health (esp. fitness and sports)
Circulation: 120,000
Distribution: Subscriptions
Editor: Terry W. Harshman
Publisher: Children's Better Health Institute
Cost: $18.95/yr. (8 issues)
Sample: $1.25 to the editorial address
Readers' Work Published: Drawings, poems, jokes, riddles

Editorial & Ordering Address:
Children's Better Health Institute
1100 Waterway Boulevard
P.O. Box 567
Indianapolis, IN 46206
317-636-8881
Fax: 317-684-8094

Children's World

Audience: M/F, ages 6–18 (English knowing)
Subject: Fact and fiction that enhances mental, emotional, and moral growth, making a well-informed reader
Circulation: 25,000
Distribution: Homes (65%); schools (25%); agents (10%)
Editor: Mrs. Vaijayanti Tonpe
Publisher: Vaijayanti Tonpe for Children's Book Trust
Cost: $7.00/issue; $75.00/yr. subscription
Sample: Contact Circulation Dept. for sample issue (free)
Readers' Work Published: Letters, stories, poems

was started in 1968 to give the creative urge in children an outlet. This 56–64 page magazine seeks to entertain, educate, and make growing up an exciting adventure through its stimulating stories and thought provoking articles and features. It also encourages children to write for it—giving them a much needed forum to express their views. It gives an Indian child his/her identity and a foreign reader a keen insight into the modern Indian child's mind.

Editorial & Ordering Address:
Children's Book Trust (CBT)
Nehru House
4 Bahadurshah Zafar Marg
New Delhi 110002, India
3316970-74
Fax: 91-11-3721090

Circle K Magazine

Audience: M/F, college students
Subject: College oriented
Circulation: 10,000
Distribution: Colleges (97%); libraries, homes, businesses, etc. (3%)
Editor: Nicholas K. Drake
Publisher: Circle K International
Cost: $4.00/yr. (5 issues)
Sample: 75¢ U.S. postage on SASE

is a 16-page publication distributed to members of Circle K International, the world's largest collegiate service organization. Only nonfiction articles of interest to the service-minded college student are included.

Editorial & Ordering Address:
3636 Woodview Trace
Indianapolis, IN 46268-3196
317-875-8755
Fax: 317-879-0204

The Claremont Review

Audience: M/F, ages 13–19
Subject: Literature, poetry, and fiction
Circulation: 700
Distribution: Homes, schools/classrooms, newsstands
Editor: Bill Stenson
Publisher: The Claremont Review Publishers
Cost: CAN$6.00/issue; CAN$12.00/yr. (2 issues)
Sample: Back issues $5.00
Readers' Work Published: Fiction, poetry, short plays

seeks to provide an English language literary journal for young adult writers in North America that is first class. Students aged 13–19 are invited to submit fiction, poetry, and short plays that demonstrate maturity and a high degree of editing.

Editorial & Ordering Address:
The Claremont Review Publishers
4980 Wesley Road
Victoria, BC
Canada V8Y 1Y9
604-658-5221
Fax: 604-658-5387
E-mail: aurora@IslandNet.com

Audience: M/F, ages 15+
Subject: Family
Circulation: 75,000
Distribution: Homes, news-stands
Editor: Bona Campillo
Publisher: Carolina Migoni
Cost: 5,000 pesos/yr.

Claudia

published in Spanish, is a monthly publication focusing on the family and the young couple. It features articles dealing with national and international tourism, health, ecology, fashions, beauty, cooking, decoration, arts and crafts, culture, people, and artists.

Editorial & Ordering Address:
Morelos #16-20
C.P. 06040
D.F. Mexico
521-1250
Fax: 510-0679

Audience: M/F, ages 8–14
Subject: Music/piano
Circulation: 70,000
Distribution: Schools, homes
Editor: Ann Rohner Callis
Publisher: James T. Rohner
Cost: $8.00/yr. (10 issues); group prices available
Sample: Contact editorial office
Readers' Work Published: Student compositions

Clavier's Piano Explorer

is a monthly music magazine designed for the student pianist. Normally distributed through piano teachers, this 16-page publication, illustrated with original water-colors, prints original student compositions in addition to stories about composers, features about orchestral instruments, and music-oriented puzzles and quizzes. It also includes discussions of piano study problems and a calendar of composers' birthdays.

Editorial & Ordering Address:
Accent Publishing Company
200 Northfield Road
Northfield, IL 60093
847-446-5000

Audience: M/F, ages 8–15
Subject: American history
Circulation: 36,000
Distribution: Schools, homes
Editor: Meg Chorlian
Publisher: Lyell C. Dawes
Cost: $24.95/yr. (9 issues)
Sample: Mail check for $5.70 with request to Cobblestone Publishing
Readers' Work Published: Letters, art, poems, contests

Cobblestone

a 48-page theme-related magazine, is designed to be used by teachers who seek an imaginative approach to teaching history—the people, events, and ideas that have shaped the American experience. Historical accuracy and original approaches to the theme treated in the issue make *Cobblestone* a valuable research tool.

Editorial & Ordering Address:
Cobblestone Publishing, Inc.
7 School Street
Peterborough, NH 03458
603-924-7209
Fax: 603-924-7380
E-mail: http://www.cobblestonepub.com

Coins Magazine

features basic information on coins, tokens, medals, and other numismatic items. The magazine's goal is to teach the fun of collecting without preaching.

Audience: M/F, ages 10+
Subject: Beginning and intermediate collectors
Circulation: 42,423
Distribution: Subscriptions (67%); newsstands (33%)
Editor: Robert Van Ryzin
Publisher: Rick Groth
Cost: $21.95/yr. (12 issues)
Sample: On written request
Readers' Work Published: Coin finds

Editorial & Ordering Address:
Krause Publications, Inc.
700 E. State Street
Iola, WI 54990-0001
715-445-2214
Fax: 715-445-4087

College Bound: Issues and Trends for the College Admissions Advisor

publishes college admissions information, statistics, issues, trends, and strategies for college admissions offices, high school counselors, private advisors, high school students, and parents in all 50 U.S. states and 42 nations. The newsletter includes surveys and information on out-of-state enrollment policies, financial aid outlook, scholarship information, minority recruitment, books, and videos.

Audience: M/F, high school students
Subject: Guidance and college advising
Distribution: Homes, schools, colleges
Editor: R. Craig Sautter
Publisher: College Bound Publications, Inc.
Cost: $59.00/yr. (10 issues); $99.00/2 yrs.; $69/foreign air mail
Sample: On written request

Editorial & Ordering Address:
P.O. Box 6536
Evanston, IL 60204
312-262-5810
Fax: 312-262-5810

College PreView

is designed to promote positive images, information, advice, and motivation for ethnically and culturally diverse young adults in the United States. Tips on services suitable to high school juniors and seniors, profiles of students overcoming problems to attend college, discussions of career possibilities, and lists of financial aid sources make up an average issue. The magazine also sponsors an essay contest, awarding a scholarship to the winner.

Audience: M/F, ages 16–20
Subject: Career and college information
Circulation: 600,000
Editor: Neoshia Michelle Paige
Publisher: Georgia Lee Clark, Communications Publishing Group, Inc.
Cost: $3.00/issue; $9.60/yr. (4 issues)

Editorial & Ordering Address:
Communications Publishing Group, Inc.
106 W. 11th Street
Suite 250
Kansas City, MO 64105-1806
816-221-4404
Fax: 816-221-1112

Colorado Kids

is a weekly 4-page children's section in *The Denver Post*. Articles and related activities are devoted to themes including sports, animals, the environment, books and entertainment, regional history, and issues of particular interest to those living in Colorado and the West. Student art and written works are published occasionally in *Colorado Kids*.

Editorial & Ordering Address:
The Denver Post
1560 Broadway
Denver, CO 80202
303-820-1837
Fax: 303-820-1406

Audience: M/F, ages 8–12
Subject: General interest and regional
Circulation: 365,000
Distribution: Home delivery of newspaper; classroom subscriptions
Editor: Laura Shreve
Publisher: The Denver Post
Readers' Work Published: Art, poetry, jokes, interviews

The Conqueror

is targeted at Pentecostal teens with the goal of encouraging them in their faith and motivating them to share that faith with friends. It uses stories and profiles of teens along with inspirational articles.

Editorial & Ordering Address:
United Pentecostal Church International
8855 Dunn Road
Hazelwood, MO 63042
314-837-7300
Fax: 314-837-4503

Audience: M/F, teens
Subject: Teen issues
Circulation: 6,300
Distribution: Direct mail, individual and group subscriptions
Editor: Darrel W. Johns
Publisher: General Youth Division, United Pentecostal Church International
Cost: $7.50/yr. (7 issues)
Sample: On written request

Coulicou

is a French-language version of *Chickadee Magazine*. It is designed to introduce children to the world of nature and animals and help them like reading. It includes games, experiences, recipes, and posters.

Editorial & Ordering Address:
Les Éditions Héritage Inc.
300 Avenue Arran
Saint Lambert, PQ
Canada J4R 1K5
514-875-0327
Fax: 514-672-5448

Audience: M/F, ages 4–8
Subject: Nature
Circulation: 18,200
Distribution: Homes (59%); schools (22%); libraries (2%); other (17%)
Editor: Luc Payette
Publisher: Les Éditions Héritage Inc.
Cost: $2.95/copy; $19.95/yr. (10 issues); $35.00/2 yrs.
Sample: Send a fax or call
Readers' Work Published: Letters, stories, drawings

Audience: M/F, ages 8–12
Subject: Sunday school take-home paper
Distribution: Churches, individual subscriptions
Editor: Janice K. Burton
Publisher: V. Gilbert Beers, Scripture Press Publications, Inc.
Cost: $1.89/quarter (13 issues); 52 issues/yr.
Sample: Free with SASE
Readers' Work Published: Letters, poems, testimonies, black ink drawings, etc.

Counselor

helps children understand how the truths of the Bible can be applied to everyday life experiences and to see how the truths of God's Word work out practically.

Editorial & Ordering Address:
Scripture Press Publications, Inc.
4050 Lee Vance View
Colorado Springs, CO 80918
800-708-5550
Orders: 800-323-7543

Audience: M/F, ages 10–15
Subject: Anything that can be made fun of
Circulation: 300,000
Distribution: Newsstands and subscriptions
Editor: Lou Silverstone & Andy Simmons
Publisher: Barry Rosenbloom
Cost: $1.99/issue; $16.67/yr. subscription
Sample: Mail $1.99 with issue request (check only)
Readers' Work Published: Letters only

Cracked

makes kids laugh through comic book satires of movies, TV, and trends.

Editorial Address:
Globe Communications
3 East 54th Street, 15th Floor
New York, NY 10022
212-838-7733

Ordering Address:
Cracked Subs
P.O. Box 114
Rouses Point, NY 12979-0114

Audience: M/F, ages 4–8
Subject: Entertainment and early education
Circulation: 400,000
Distribution: Homes, newsstands
Editor: Mary L. Heaton
Publisher: Deborah Jones Barrow, Meredith Custom Publishing Services
Cost: $2.95/issue; $12.97/yr. (6 issues)
Sample: $2.95/issue
Readers' Work Published: letters, artwork related to upcoming theme

Crayola Kids Magazine

is desgined to excite young children about the magic of reading and the joy of creativity. Theme issues present children's literature and related coloring, drawing, crafting, and fact-based activities as a creative and intellectual springboard for prereaders and early readers.

Editorial Address:
Meredith Custom
   Publishing Services
1912 Grand Avenue
Des Moines, IA 50309-3379
515-284-2007
515-284-2064

Ordering Address:
Crayola Kids Customer
   Service
P.O. Box 37198
Boone, IA 50037-0198
800-846-7968

Creative Kids

seeks to entertain, stimulate, and encourage the creativity of kids ages 8–14. The magazine includes stories, poetry, games, artwork, photography, and opinion, all by kids. Plus, every issue includes an invitation for kids to be published.

Audience: M/F, ages 8–14
Subject: Stories, artwork, games, opinion, poetry
Circulation: 45,000
Distribution: Homes, schools
Editor: Libby Lindsey
Publisher: Joel McIntosh
Cost: $19.95/yr. (4 issues)
Sample: Call 800-998-2208 or send $3.00 to editorial address
Readers' Work Published: Poems, stories, games, artwork, photography

Editorial & Ordering Address:
Prufrock Press
P.O. Box 8813
Waco, TX 76714-8813
800-998-2208
Fax: 800-240-0333
E-mail: Creative_kid@prufrock.com

Creative with Words Publications

encourages writers, both children and adults, to be creative with the English word, to be brief, and to approach a subject from a different perspective.

Audience: M/F, young adults, adults
Subject: Writings of children, folkloristic items, nature, humor
Distribution: Homes (80%); schools (5%); libraries (5%); universities (5%)
Editor: Brigitta Geltrich
Publisher: Creative with Words Publications
Cost: $12.00/issue; 12 issues/yr.
Sample: Children's issue $6.00; adult issue $6.00
Readers' Work Published: Stories, poems, language art

Editorial & Ordering Address:
Creative with Words Publications
P.O. Box 223226
Carmel, CA 93922
Fax: 408-655-8627

Cricket Magazine

offers a wide variety of stories and illustrations to help young people develop an appreciation for good writing and art. *Cricket* inspires, informs, and entertains in a lively, nondidactic fashion. It stimulates young readers' sense of wonder and respect for nature; it introduces children to many cultures and customs from antiquity to the present, respecting children's intelligence and never talking down to them.

Audience: M/F, ages 9–14
Subject: Fiction, nonfiction, and art
Circulation: 80,000
Distribution: Homes, schools
Editor: Marianne Carus
Publisher: Robert W. Harper
Cost: $32.97/yr. (12 issues)
Sample: $4.00; contact editor
Readers' Work Published: Must comply with monthly topic outlined in issue

Editorial Address:
Carus Publishing
315 Fifth Street
P.O. Box 300
Peru, IL 61354
815-223-1500

Ordering Address:
P.O. Box 7433
Red Oak, IA 51591-4433
800-827-0227

Crusader

is for Calvinist Cadets and their friends. It is designed to help pre-teen and early teenage boys see how God is at work in their lives and in the world around them.

Audience: M, ages 9–14
Subject: Christian life
Circulation: 13,000
Distribution: Subscriptions
Editor: G. Richard Broene
Publisher: Calvinist Cadet Corps
Cost: $7.00/yr. (7 issues)
Sample: Send 9" × 12" SASE with 3 U.S. first-class stamps

Editorial & Ordering Address:
Calvinist Cadet Corps
P.O. Box 7259
Grand Rapids, MI 49510
616-241-5616
Fax: 616-241-5558

Current Events

is designed to bring the latest U.S. national and international news to students in grades 7–10. It is concise enough to be used in a single class period, and it seeks to supply sufficient background for students to understand the central issues and events of the day. Through its skills pages, *Current Events* uses the news to help teachers teach basic social studies skills.

Audience: M/F, grades 7–10
Subject: News
Circulation: 200,000
Distribution: Schools
Editor: Charles A. Piddock
Publisher: Richard J. LeBrasseur
Cost: $7.25/subscription for 10 or more sets
Sample: Contact Bob Pfister at the ordering address

Editorial Address:
Weekly Reader Corp.
P.O. Box 2791
Middletown, CT 06457-9291
860-638-2400
Fax: 860-346-5964

Ordering Address:
Weekly Reader Corp.
3001 Cindel Drive
Delran, NJ 08370
800-446-3355

Current Health I

is a 32-page classroom magazine designed for middle grade students. It focuses on health education. Topics include nutrition, first aid and safety, fitness and exercise, drugs, and disease.

Audience: M/F, grades 4–7
Subject: Health education
Circulation: 146,992
Distribution: Schools
Editor: Carole Rubenstein
Publisher: Richard J. LeBrasseur
Cost: $8.25/subscription for 15 or more sets (9 issues)

Editorial Address:
GLC
900 Skokie Boulevard
Suite 200
Northbrook, IL 60062-4028

Ordering Address:
Weekly Reader Corp.
3001 Cindel Drive
Delran, NJ 08370
800-446-3355

Current Health II

Audience: M/F, grades 7–12
Subject: Health education
Circulation: 222,232
Distribution: Schools
Editor: Carole Rubenstein
Publisher: Richard J. LeBrasseur
Cost: $8.25/subscription for 15 or more sets

serves high school students in the health education area. Designed as a supplement to the classroom text, this 32-page magazine deals with health-oriented issues including new research and discoveries. The Human Sexuality Supplement focuses on concerns in the area of sex education and includes the most current information on human sexuality.

Editorial Address:
GLC
900 Skokie Boulevard
Suite 200
Northbrook, IL 60062-4028

Ordering Address:
Weekly Reader Corp.
3001 Cindel Drive
Delran, NJ 08370
800-446-3355

Current Science

Audience: M/F, grades 7–9
Subject: Science
Circulation: 311,996
Distribution: Schools
Publisher: Richard J. LeBrasseur
Cost: $7.45/subscription for 10 or more sets
Sample: Contact customer service

presents current news in science, health, and technology to middle school and junior high school readers. It attempts to relate science to kids while challenging their critical thinking. Other features include science activities, U.S. national science projects, science mystery photos, and kids in the news. The 16-page bimonthly is in its sixth decade of publication.

Editorial Address:
GLC
900 Skokie Boulevard
Suite 200
Northbrook, IL 60062-4028

Ordering Address:
Weekly Reader Corp.
3001 Cindel Drive
Delran, NJ 08370
800-446-3355

Das Rad

Audience: M/F, ages 11–16
Subject: German language, sports, TV, film, culture
Distribution: Schools
Editor: Miroslav Imbresevic
Publisher: Mary Glasgow Magazines
Cost: $6.95/subscription (6 issues)
Sample: Available from ordering address
Readers' Work Published: Letters, artwork, photos

is written in German for teenagers learning German at school. It covers topics of interest to the age group, at the same time introducing information and cultural details so that readers learn about the language and background of the countries where German is spoken. Its goal is to make German come alive for its readers.

Editorial Address:
Mary Glasgow Magazines
Commonwealth House
1–19 New Oxford Street
London, England WC1A 1NU
441-71-4219050
Fax: 441-71-4219052

Ordering Address:
Scholastic Inc.
2931 East McCarty Street
P.O. Box 3710
Jefferson City, MO 65102-3710

The Daybreak Star Indian Reader

Audience: M/F, grades 4–6
Subject: Native American history, tribal lifestyles, practices, and values
Circulation: 4,500
Distribution: Schools (85%); libraries (10%); homes (5%)
Editor: Kathryn Oneita
Publisher: United Indians of All Tribes Foundation
Cost: $5.75/issue for 2–10 subscriptions (8 issues)
Sample: On written request
Readers' Work Published: Native children's artwork, letters, stories, puzzles, legends

a 24-page magazine, features accurate information about native Amercians and their cultures. Each of the eight issues has a regional focus (NW, SW, Plains, etc.) with a change in theme (such as ceremonialism or government) each year. The *Reader* blends historical and contemporary facts about tribal lifestyles, practices, and values.

Editorial & Ordering Address:
United Indians of All Tribes Foundation
1945 Yale Place E.
Seattle, WA 98102
206-325-0070
Fax: 206-328-1608

Devo'Zine

Audience: M/F, ages 12–18
Subject: Real-life issues of youth, spiritual growth, prayer, humor, media reviews, environment, profiles of famous and ordinary people
Circulation: 25,000
Distribution: Churches (80%); homes (20%)
Editor: Robin R. Pippin
Publisher: Janice T. Grana
Cost: $16.95/yr.
Sample: Send SASE (6" × 8") with 4 1st class stamps to editorial address
Readers' Work Published: Short meditations, feature articles

seeks to help youth develop a lifetime pattern of prayer and spiritual reflection. Supported by scripture and written by youth and adults who care about youth, these daily meditations and weekend feature articles explore the relevancy of the Christian faith for readers' lives. This 64-page, 4-color, bimonthly magazine began with the May/June 1996 issue.

Editorial Address:
The Upper Room
1908 Grand Avenue
P.O. Box 189
Nashville, TN 37202
615-340-7247
Fax: 615-340-7006
E-mail: 102615.3145@compuserve.com

Ordering Address:
Devo'Zine
P.O. Box 37140
Boone, IA 50037-0140
800-925-6847

Audience: M/F, visually impaired students and adults seeking career and recreational information
Subject: First person experiences with sports and recreation, skills used for daily life, poetry and fiction.
Circulation: 1,000
Distribution: Individuals (60%); libraries/agencies for the blind (30%); schools (10%)
Editor: Carol M. McCarl
Publisher: Blindskills, Inc.
Cost: $25.00/yr.
Sample: $6.00 per copy

Dialogue, A World of Ideas for Visually Impaired People of All Ages

is for visually impaired students and adults seeking career and recreational information.

Editorial & Ordering Address:
Blindskills, Inc.
P.O. Box 5181
Salem, OR 97304
503-581-4224
Fax: 503-581-0178

Audience: M/F, ages 7–14
Subject: Adventure, entertainment, science, puzzles, games
Circulation: 1 million
Editor: Phyllis Ehrlich
Publisher: Peter Medwid
Cost: $2.99/issue; $19.95/yr. (12 issues)
Sample: Request in writing plus check for $2.99
Readers' Work Published: Occasional contests for scary stories, or stories on super heroes, villains, etc.

Disney Adventures

is a general interest magazine for kids ages 7–14. It appeals to the scope of a kid's imagination by featuring articles and departments covering entertainment, sports, science, travel, comics, puzzles, and much more. *Disney Adventures'* primary goal is to attract kids to reading as entertainment.

Editorial Address:
Disney Adventures
   Magazine
114 Fifth Avenue
New York, NY 10011-5690
212-807-5821
Fax: 212-807-5499
E-mail: dazpc@aol.com

Ordering Address:
Suite 101 at editorial
address
818-973-4173
800-829-5146
Fax: 818-559-7353

Audience: M/F, ages 7–13
Subject: Environmentalism, marine biology, general science
Circulation: 60,000
Distribution: Membership only (home and school)
Editor: Lisa Rao
Publisher: The Cousteau Society
Cost: $2.50/issue; $15.00/yr. (6 issues)
Sample: Send check for $2.00 and 9" × 12" SASE with 3 U.S. 1st class stamps to the Cousteau Society

Dolphin Log

seeks to delight, instruct, and instill in children an environmental ethic, including an understanding of the interconnectedness of all living organisms. *Dolphin Log* is the Cousteau Society's nonfiction publication for children. This 20-page bimonthly encompasses science, marine biology, and the environment as they relate to our global water system.

Editorial Address:
The Cousteau Society
777 United Nations Plaza
New York, NY 10017
212-949-6290
Fax: 212-949-6296

Ordering Address:
The Cousteau Society
870 Greenbrier Circle
Suite 402
Chesapeake, VA 23320
804-523-9335

Dramatics

seeks to provide practical information to help students and teachers make better theater. It attempts to help students make an informed decision about whether to pursue a theater career and how to prepare for it. Finally, it seeks to equip students for lifelong appreciation of performing arts.

Audience: M/F, high school students and teachers
Subject: Performing arts
Circulation: 35,500
Distribution: Homes (90%); classrooms (10%)
Editor: Don Corathers
Publisher: Educational Theatre Association
Cost: $2.50/issue; $18.00/yr. (9 issues)
Sample: Send $3.50 or SASE with $1.24 U.S. postage

Editorial & Ordering Address:
3368 Central Parkway
Cincinnati, OH 45225
513-559-1996
Fax: 513-559-0012
E-mail: info@etassol.org

EarthSavers

is the quarterly newspaper of the EarthSavers program, an environmental club program for kids and their adult leaders, coordinated by the National Wildlife Federation and sponsored by Target Stores. The newspaper is designed to help members learn more about nature and wildlife, experience the wonders of the outdoors, and improve and protect the natural environment of their communities.

Audience: M/F, ages 6–13
Subject: Wildlife conservation, environment
Circulation: 485,000
Distribution: Club members (1%); remainder free at Target stores
Editor: Betsy Wooster
Publisher: National Wildlife Federation
Cost: Free (4 issues/yr.)
Sample: Write to editorial office; free + club registration form
Readers' Work Published: Letters

Editorial & Ordering Address:
National Wildlife Federation
8925 Leesburg Pike
Vienna, VA 22184
703-790-4535

Edge: The High Performance Electronic Magazine for Students

chronicles the "learning lifestyle" for teenagers, turning teenagers on to the many opportunities for alternative learning experiences available to them, such as a wilderness trip to Alberta. Published bimonthly.

Audience: M/F, ages 14–17
Subject: Anything related to the "learning lifestyle"
Distribution: World Wide Web
Editor: Greg Sanders
Publisher: Webb Howell
Readers' Work Published: Opinion or point-of-view essays

Editorial & Ordering Address:
Journalistic, Inc.
4905 Pine Cove Drive, Suite #2
Durham, NC 27707
919-489-1916
Fax: 919-489-4767
E-mail: gsanders@interpath.com

Audience: M/F, ages 11–16
Subject: Spanish language, sports, TV, film, pop, teen culture, Spanish and Latin American cultures
Circulation: 90,000
Distribution: Schools for classroom-home usage
Editor: Marta Gidings
Publisher: Mary Glasgow Magazines
Cost: $6.95/school yr.
Sample: Contact Scholastic Inc.
Readers' Work Published: Letters, artwork, photos

El Sol

is written in Spanish for teenagers learning Spanish at school. It covers topics of interest to the age group, at the same time introducing information and cultural details so that readers learn the language and background of the countries where Spanish is spoken. Its goal is to make Spanish come alive for its readers.

Editorial Address:
Mary Glasgow Magazines
Commonwealth House
1–19 New Oxford Street
London, England WC1A 1NU
441-71-4219050
Fax: 441-71-4219052

Ordering Address:
Scholastic Classroom Magazines
2931 East McCarty Street
P.O. Box 3710
Jefferson City, MO 65102-3710

Audience: M/F, ages 7–13
Circulation: 8,000
Distribution: Homes (20%); schools (80%)
Cost: 75 mk/school year
Readers' Work Published: Letters, stories, and artwork

Eos

teaches children the positive side of sports and other interests. It also deals with the harmful effects of drugs.

Editorial & Ordering Address:
Fredsgatan 8B
Finlands Svenska Nykterhetsforbund
65100 Vasa, Finland
961-3172604
Fax: 961-3172831

Audience: M/F, ages 8–14
Subject: World cultures
Circulation: 13,000
Distribution: Schools, homes
Editor: Carolyn P. Yoder
Publisher: Lyell C. Dawes, Cobblestone Publishing, Inc.
Cost: $23.95/yr. (9 issues)
Sample: Mail check for $5.70 with request to Cobblestone Publishing, Inc.
Readers' Work Published: Letters, art, poems, contests

Faces

is a theme-related magazine that seeks to explore human diversity and fosters respect for people of other cultures. Working with the anthropology department of the American Museum of Natural History, the editorial staff introduces readers to the many lifestyles, beliefs, and customs found throughout the world.

Editorial & Ordering Address:
Cobblestone Publishing, Inc.
7 School Street
Peterborough, NH 03458
603-924-7209
Fax: 603-924-7380
E-mail: http://www.cobblestonepub.com

Falcon Magazine

was founded on the belief that too many kids today lack a realistic connection to the natural world. This conservation magazine emphasizes the importance of wildlife, healthy habitat, and the significance of all living things in the web of life. *Falcon Magazine* encourages kids to "make a difference" in protecting our natural resources. The focus is largely North American.

Editorial & Ordering Address:
Two Worlds Publishing
3060 Peachtree Road, NW
Suite 500
Atlanta, GA 30305
404-262-8921

Audience: M/F, ages 8–12
Subject: Nature, conservation, wildlife, outdoor activities
Circulation: 1.2 million
Distribution: Homes (66%)
Editor: Vickie Favorite
Publisher: Two Worlds, Harold Chambliss
Cost: $14.95 (6 issues)
Sample: $3.95 with SASE
Readers' Work Published: Book reviews, "Short Stuff," "Making a Difference" (nominate your favorite)

Fantastic Flyer Magazine

is an integral part of Delta Airlines' interactive marketing program for children ages 2–12. The program seeks to encourage geography literacy through a love of travel, an interest in reading, and a feeling of belonging. Regular features introduce readers to children around the world who share the same interests but whose lands, customs, art, language, and science may differ.

Editorial & Ordering Address:
Delta Airlines, Inc.
Department 790, Admin. Bldg.
1030 Delta Boulevard
Atlanta, GA 30320
404-715-4813

Audience: M/F, ages 2–12
Circulation: 1.1 million
Distribution: Homes (60%); airplanes (40%)
Editor: Margaret Stack Ross
Publisher: Delta Air Lines, Inc.
Cost: Free to program members
Readers' Work Published: Letters, art, jokes, stories

FFA New Horizons

informs Future Farmers of America members of newest developments and opportunities in agricultural careers, FFA, education, and recreation.

Editorial & Ordering Address:
National FFA Organization
5632 Mt. Vernon Memorial Highway
Alexandria, VA 22309
703-360-3600

Audience: M/F, high school students
Subject: Careers, general youth issues, college, outdoor recreation
Circulation: 430,000
Distribution: Homes
Editor: Lawinna McGary
Publisher: Future Farmers of America
Cost: $3.50 (6 issues)
Sample: Write or call the office
Readers' Work Published: Cartoons, articles on members

Field & Stream, Jr.

Audience: M/F, ages 8–12
Subject: Hunting and fishing
Circulation: 2 million
Distribution: Contained in
Field & Stream approxi-
mately every other month
Editor: Duncan Barnes
Publisher: Michael Rooney
Cost: $2.50/issue

is a 3-page bimonthly section of *Field & Stream*. The goal of *Jr.* is to pass on the traditions of hunting and fishing to the up-and-coming generation. It features how-to articles but also covers natural history and conservation—all with a hunting or fishing focus.

No longer published

Editorial & Ordering Address:
Times Mirror Magazines, Inc.
2 Park Avenue
New York, NY
212-779-5000
Fax: 212-725-3836
E-mail: FSmagazine@aol.com
Orders: 212-779-5000

FineScale Modeler

Audience: M, young adult,
adult
Subject: Static models—
airplanes, tanks, cars,
ships, figures, dioramas
Circulation: 80,000
Distribution: Subscriptions,
hobby shops, bookstores
Editor: Bob Hayden
Publisher: Kalmbach
Publishing Co.
Cost: $32.95/yr.

is devoted to the hobby of scale modeling. Its readership includes those interested in building the diverse models it features. The magazine centers on how-to-do-it techniques with photos and drawings designed to assist the beginning and more advanced modeler.

Editorial Address:
21027 Crossroads Circle
Waukesha, WI 53187
414-796-8776
Fax: 414-796-0126
E-mail: customerservice@kalmbach.com

Ordering Address:
P.O. Box 1612
Waukesha, WI 53187
800-533-6644
Fax: 414-796-0126

First Opportunity

Audience: M/F, ages 16+
Subject: Planning for higher
education in technology
and science
Circulation: 500,000
Editor: Georgia Lee Clark
Publisher: Georgia Lee Clark,
Communications
Publishing Group, Inc.
Cost: $3.00/issue; $9.60/yr.
(4 issues)

is designed to promote positive images, information, advice, and motivation for ethnically and culturally diverse youths and young adults in the United States. Tips on services suitable to technology- and science-minded high school students, discussions of career possibilities, and lists of financial aid sources make up an average issue.

Editorial & Ordering Address:
Communications Publishing Group, Inc.
106 W. 11th Street
Suite 250
Kansas City, MO 64105-1806
816-221-4404
Fax: 816-221-1112

Flohkiste (Fleabag) Grade 1

Audience: M/F, grades 1–5 (four editions)
Publisher: Domino Verlag, Günther Brinek
Cost: DM 114 (including postage in Germany) (30 issues)

(1st and 2nd grade editions) are magazines supporting the curriculum of German schools and are designed to be used in class as a curriculum supplement. These magazines are linked to *Floh* youth magazines for children in 3rd and 4th grades and from the 5th grade and up. Enclosed with *Floh* is the newspaper "Hallo Walt" with political and social news.

Editorial & Ordering Address:
Domino Verlag Gunther Brinek GmbH
Menzinger Strasse 13
80638 München
Germany
089-17913-0

For Graduates Only

Audience: M/F, ages 18–21
Subject: Guidance for students graduating from 2-year colleges
Circulation: 100,000
Distribution: By written request from transfer/ career counselor
Editor: Judi Oliff
Publisher: Darryl G. Elberg
Cost: Free to schools; $2.00/issue to individuals
Sample: On written request

is edited to provide students graduating from 2-year community, junior, and technical colleges with information on options available to them. Options treated include continuing their education or transferring to a four-year college, obtaining additional vocational or technical education, seeking employment, or joining a branch of the military.

Editorial & Ordering Address:
Campus Communications, Inc.
339 N. Main Street
New City, NY 10956
914-638-0333

For Seniors Only

Audience: M/F, ages 16–19
Subject: Career guide articles, college selections, financial aid
Circulation: 350,000
Distribution: Schools by written request from guidance counselor
Editor: Judi Oliff
Publisher: Darryl G. Elberg
Cost: $2.00/issue
Sample: On written request

seeks to provide its readers with methods for succeeding in college, summer job opportunities, information on scholarships and financial assistance, opportunities in the various branches of the military, specialized career training, and tips on how to find a job. Other features include worksheets for calculating college expenses, directions on preparing résumés, and instructions on how to write letters to receive information.

Editorial & Ordering Address:
Campus Communications, Inc.
339 N. Main Street
New City, NY 10956
914-638-0333

*Audience: M/F, high school
students*
*Subject: Christian articles and
essays*
*Publisher: Scripture Press
Publications, Inc.*

Freeway

seeks to show readers how principles for Christian living can be applied in their everyday lives and in crisis situations. The publication uses true-to-life fiction, true stories, self-help articles, puzzles, and poetry to teach biblical truths.

Editorial Address:
Scripture Press
   Publications, Inc.
Box 632
Glen Ellyn, IL 60183
708-668-6000
Fax: 708-668-3806

Ordering Address:
Scripture Press
   Publications, Inc.
1825 College Avenue
Wheaton, IL 60187
800-323-9409

*Audience: M/F, keen readers
ages 12 and up*
*Subject: All aspects of world
history*
Circulation: 35,000
*Distribution: Homes (75%);
schools (20%); newsagents/
bookshops (5%)*
Editor: Dr. Franz Metzger
*Publisher: Hermann
Uebelherr*
*Cost: DM 6,40/issue;
DM 76,80/yr.*
*Sample: See ordering address;
single sample and informa-
tion leaflet free*

G—Geschichte mit Pfiff (History with Pizazz)

offers academically solid knowledge about world history with an entertaining approach and easy reading.

Editorial & Ordering Address:
Auesserer Laufer Platz 22
Sailer Verlag
D-90327 Nurnberg, Germany
911-5396655
Fax: 911-5396912

Audience: F, ages 7–14
*Subject: Sports, food, crafts,
entertainment*
Circulation: 150,000
*Distribution: Subscriptions,
newsstands*
*Editor: Kelly White and
Michelle Silver*
Publisher: Karen Bokram
Cost: $2.95/issue; $14.95/yr.
Sample: $5.00
*Readers' Work Published:
Some stories, poems, and
artwork*

Girls' Life

is a national magazine for girls ages 7–14 with the philosophy that every piece of art and every article written reinforces the idea that girls are important, independent, opinionated people. This magazine inspires confidence in every girl and is unique, fun, and informative.

Editorial & Ordering Address:
Monarch Publishing
4517 Harford Rd.
Baltimore, MD 21214
410-254-9200
Fax: 410-254-0991

The Goldfinch

Audience: M/F, ages 8–13
Subject: Iowa history
Circulation: 1,500
Distribution: Homes (50%); schools (50%)
Editor: Amy Ruth
Cost: $10.00/yr. (4 issues)
Sample: $4.00
Readers' Work Published: Letters, stories, artwork, poems

is an Iowa history magazine for children ages 8–13. Each 32-page issue is theme based, exploring one theme or aspect of Iowa history. *The Goldfinch* publishes feature articles, original historical fiction, history-in-the-news features, as well as games, puzzles, and contests. It also publishes readers' poetry, short essays, and artwork. All writers are encouraged to send a SASE for writer's guidelines before submitting to *The Goldfinch*.

Editorial & Ordering Address:
State Historical Society of Iowa
402 Iowa Avenue
Iowa City, IA 52240
319-335-3930

Grain de Soleil

Audience: M/F, ages 8–12
Subject: Religious culture and faith in news features
Circulation: 80,000
Distribution: Subscriptions, schools, newsstands
Editor: Emmanuelle Dalyac
Publisher: Bayard Presse
Cost: 29 FF/issue; 289 FF/yr.

is for children who are curious about God and is the ideal companion in helping to encourage an awakening of religious culture and faith. *Grain de Soleil* deals with a wide range of subjects through its news features, historical fact files, cartoons, and illustrations. Every quarter, there's a liturgical supplement that helps children improve their understanding of the mass.

Editorial Address:
Bayard Presse
3 rue Bayard
Paris 75008, France
331-44-356060
Fax: 331-44-35604

Ordering Address:
Bayard Presse International
BP 12
99505 Paris Entreprise France
331-44-216000

Guide Magazine

Audience: M/F, ages 10–14
Subject: Christian living
Circulation: 40,000
Distribution: Church handouts; individual subscriptions
Editor: Carolyn Rathbun
Publisher: Review & Herald Publishing Association
Cost: $36.97/yr. (52 issues)
Sample: Send business size SASE for free copy
Readers' Work Published: Letters, artwork, opinions (response to special columns)

aims to reflect both editorially and graphically the unconditional love of God. In so doing, the magazine hopes to foster a greater sense of self-worth, assurance, and concern for others. The content seeks to be highly needs-responsive, reflecting a young person's perspective, both physically and intellectually, with a fun, dynamic, contemporary look.

Editorial & Ordering Address:
Review & Herald Publishing Association
55 W. Oak Ridge Drive
Hagerstown, MD 21740
301-791-7000, ext. 2433
Fax: 301-790-9734
E-mail: 74617.3100@compuserve.com

Audience: M/F, ages 7–12
Subject: Values centered
Circulation: 200,000+
Distribution: Subscriptions
Editor: Mary Lou Carney
Publisher: Guideposts
Cost: $2.95/issue; $15.95/yr. (6 issues)
Sample: Write to Guideposts, 39 Seminary Hill Rd., Carmel, NY 10512

Guideposts for Kids

is a fun, value-centered, bimonthly magazine created to help kids learn how to think rather than what to think. It takes kids' problems seriously—everything from divorce to D's in math to friendship dilemmas—and strives to help kids develop their own coping skills. Each issue contains true stories, many of which are adapted from the parent magazine *Guideposts*. Issue-oriented, entertaining, age and interest appropriate, based on moral principles—are the editorial objectives.

Editorial Address:
Guideposts
P.O. Box 538A
Chesterton, IN 46304
219-929-4429
Fax: 219-926-3839

Ordering Address:
Guideposts
P.O. Box 1419
Carmel, NY 10512-9869

Audience: M/F, ages 3–5
Subject: Stories, activities, songs related to Christian nurture
Circulation: 37,000
Distribution: Bulk subscriptions through church schools and congregations (90%); individual subscriptions (10%)
Editor: Dr. Earl H. Gaulke
Publisher: Concordia Publishing House
Cost: 99¢/issue; $7.75/yr.; bulk rates available
Sample: Call Concordia Publishing House 800-325-3040

Happy Times

is designed for 3- to 5-year olds and includes stories, songs, poems, puzzles, and projects, all with a biblical foundation to appeal to both children and parents. Sunday school and preschool teachers can use *Happy Times* to provide children with ready-made activities that reinforce a Bible lesson.

Editorial & Ordering Address:
Concordia Publishing House
3558 S. Jefferson Avenue
St. Louis, MO 63118
314-268-1000
Fax: 314-268-1329

Audience: M/F, ages 7–14
Subject: African American experience
Circulation: 7,000
Distribution: Schools (90%); libraries (10%)
Editor: Wade Hudson
Publisher: Wade Hudson
Cost: $15.00 (3 issues)
Sample: Send SASE ($1.52) to publisher
Readers' Work Published: Letters, stories, games, photographs

Harambee

is designed to help youngsters better understand the African and African American history and culture. Contemporary issues are covered, and each issue focuses on a specific theme or aspect of the black experience.

Editorial & Ordering Address:
Just Us Books, Inc.
356 Glenwood Avenue
East Orange, NJ 07017
201-676-4345
Fax: 201-677-7570

Audience: M/F, ages 8–13
Subject: Nature
Circulation: 21,500
Distribution: Homes (62%);
schools (22%); libraries
(2%); other (14%)
Editor: Sylvie Payette
Publisher: Les Éditions
Héritage Inc.
Cost: CAN$2.99/copy;
CAN$20.95 (10 issues)
Sample: Send a fax or call
Readers' Work Published:
Letters, stories, drawings,
answers to questions

Hibou

is a French language adaptation of *Owl Magazine,* "The Discovery Magazine for Kids." Like *Owl,* its mandate is to inform and interest kids ages 8 and up in science, nature, and the world around them. *Hibou* challenges kids to see everyday things in new ways by showcasing the best in photography, illustration, ideas, and activities.

Editorial & Ordering Address:
Les Éditions Héritage Inc.
300 Avenue Arran
Saint Lambert, PQ
Canada J4R 1K5
514-875-0327
Fax: 514-672-5448

Audience: M, ages 5–17
Subject: Camping, adventure,
devotions, how-to's for boys
Circulation: 86,000
Distribution: Chartering,
subscriptions
Editor: Marshall Bruner
Publisher: Gospel Publishing
House
Cost: $1.75/yr.
Sample: Send 8½" × 11"
SASE with request

High Adventure

is a quarterly Royal Rangers magazine for boys. This 16-page, 4-color periodical is designed to provide boys with worthwhile, enjoyable leisure reading; to challenge them to higher ideals and greater spiritual dedication; and to perpetuate the spirit of the Royal Rangers program through stories, ideas, crafts, and illustrations.

Editorial Address:
Gospel Publishing House
Royal Rangers Department
1445 Boonville Avenue
Springfield, MO 65802
417-862-8558

Ordering Address:
Customer Service
1445 Boonville Avenue
Springfield, MO 65802

Audience: M/F, ages 2–12
Subject: General interest
Circulation: 3,000,000
Distribution: Homes
Editor: Kent L. Brown, Jr.
Publisher: Highlights for
Children, Inc.
Cost: $21.95/yr. (11 issues)
Sample: Send SASE to
editorial address
Readers' Work Published:
Poems, drawings, stories
(under 200 words), letters
to the editor

Highlights for Children

is a 42-page general interest magazine whose motto is "Fun with a Purpose." Each issue has crafts, verse, and thinking features interspersed among short stories and factual articles. *Highlights* accepts original poems, short prose, drawings, and questions about science or personal problems (from children through age 15). It also accepts jokes and riddles that need not be original.

Editorial Address:
803 Church Street
Honesdale, PA 18431
717-253-1080
Fax: 717-253-0179

Ordering Address:
P.O. Box 269
Columbus, OH 43272-0002
800-848-8922

HiP Magazine

is first and foremost a magazine for kids who also happen to have a hearing loss. Its colorful and fun format provides opportunities for kids to strengthen their educational and social skills through reading, a universal mode of communication for deaf and hearing impaired kids. *HiP* also assists children in educating others about hearing loss issues and shows how everyday experiences and exceptional achievements are within every child's grasp.

Audience: M/F, all deaf and hard-of-hearing children, ages 8–14
Subject: General interest
Circulation: 10,000
Distribution: Subscriptions only to schools, teachers (50%); children (30%); hearing care professionals (20%)
Editor: Ellen Dolich and Robin Gladstone
Publisher: Ellen Dolich and Robin Gladstone
Cost: $3.50/issue, $14.95/yr.
Sample: Contact ordering address
Readers' Work Published: Letters, stories, artwork, responses to magazine questions, and a personal profile called "All About Me."

Editorial Address:
HiP Magazine
127 Seabridge Court
Alameda, California 94502
510-523-4221
Fax: 510-523-4081

Ordering Address:
HiP Magazine
1563 Solano Avenue #137
Berkeley, CA 94707
510-527-8993

Hit Parader

seeks to cover the most popular artists in rock music and to give insights about their music, attitudes, and everything else that goes into making each artist special.

Audience: M/F, young adult
Subject: Music—popular, heavy metal
Distribution: Newsstands, subscriptions
Editor: Andy Secher
Cost: $3.95/issue; $29.50/yr. (12 issues)
Readers' Work Published: Letters

Editorial & Ordering Address:
210 Route 4E
Suite 401
Paramus, NJ 07652
201-843-4004
Orders: 800-403-5791

Hobson's Choice

tries to show its readers the link between science fiction and fact by complementing short stories with articles on current technology. A recent issue, for example, paired a story about androids on a distant planet with an article on NASA's experimental robots.

Audience: M/F, ages 13+
Subject: Science fiction, technology
Circulation: 2,000
Distribution: Subscriptions (100%)
Editor: Susannah C. West
Publisher: David F. Powell
Cost: $2.00/issue; $12.00/yr. (6 issues)
Sample: Available for $2.50

Editorial & Ordering Address:
Starwind Press
P.O. Box 98
Ripley, OH 45167
513-392-4549

Audience: M/F, families with children ages 6–12
Subject: Daily devotional readings based on Lutheran lectionary
Circulation: 70,000
Distribution: Subscriptions (90%); other (10%)
Editor: Randy Griner
Publisher: Augsburg Fortress
Cost: $1.70/issue; $5.10/yr. (4 issues)
Sample: Free sample on request; send 6" × 9" SASE

The Home Altar

is intended to aid families with children in the practice of reading the Bible, reflecting on their life of faith, and praying together every day. This devotional periodical suggests a short passage of scripture for families to read aloud together, offers a short meditation or prayer, and provides a concluding prayer.

Editorial & Ordering Address:
Augsburg Fortress
426 South Fifth Street
Box 1209
Minneapolis, MN 55440
800-328-4648

Audience: F, ages 6–12
Subject: General interest for girls (nature, sports, hobbies, fiction)
Circulation: 9,000
Distribution: Schools and libraries (80%); subscriptions (20%)
Editor: Marilyn Edwards
Publisher: The Bluffton News Publishing and Printing Company
Cost: $15.00/yr. (6 issues); $27.50/2 yrs.
Sample: $3.00
Readers' Work Published: Potsy's Post Office (letters to the editor), contests

Hopscotch: The Magazine for Young Girls

is designed to stretch imaginations and inspire more reading, and strives to challenge girls to enjoy and make the utmost use of those few and precious years of childhood before they are forced into the turbulent and complicated cauldron known as young adulthood. It showcases young girls involved in different and worthwhile activities, encouraging its readers to engage in similar endeavors.

Editorial & Ordering Address:
P.O. Box 164
Bluffton, OH 45817-0164
419-358-4610
Fax: 419-358-5027

Audience: M/F, ages 13–19
Subject: Vegetarian living; environmental, animal, global issues, and activism
Circulation: 1,300
Distribution: Homes (90%); schools (10%)
Editor: Sally Clinton
Publisher: Vegetarian Education Network
Cost: $3.00/issue; $12.00/yr. (4 issues)
Sample: Send SASE with 2 U.S. 1st class stamps
Readers' Work Published: HOE! is almost entirely written by teens.

How On Earth!: Youth Supporting Compassionate, Ecologically Sound Living

advocates compassionate, ecologically sound living among youth. Its goal is to serve as a support network among vegetarian teens and others concerned about animal, environmental, and global issues. *HOE!* is not only for teens, but by teens. Also featured is a vegetarian nutrition column by a registered dietician, recipes, and ideas for activism.

Editorial & Ordering Address:
Vegetarian Education Network
P.O. Box 339
Oxford, PA 19363-0339
717-529-8638
Fax: 717-529-3000
E-mail: howonearth@aol.com

Audience: M/F, ages 4–6
Subject: General interest, health
Distribution: Homes
Editor: Sandra J. Grieshop
Publisher: Children's Better Health Institute
Cost: $15.95/yr. (8 issues)
Sample: Teachers and librarians send $1.25 to editorial address
Readers' Work Published: Readers' drawings

Humpty Dumpty

is a general interest magazine with an emphasis on health. It contains illustrated stories, articles, and poems for beginning readers and prereaders. Activity pages include games, dot-to-dots, hidden pictures, mazes, and simple word puzzles. Easy-to-make crafts and simple, healthful recipes are regular features.

Editorial & Ordering Address:
Children's Better Health Institute
1100 Waterway Boulevard
P.O. Box 567
Indianapolis, IN 46206
317-636-8881
Fax: 317-684-8094

Audience: F, ages 17–22
Subject: Hair, beauty, health, fashion
Circulation: 100,000
Distribution: Newsstands, subscriptions
Editor: Adrienne Moore
Publisher: Word Up! Publications
Cost: $3.99/issue (6 issues)

Hype Hair

seeks to present how-to hairstyling techniques. The aim of *Hype Hair* is to give an overall view of the great diversity in which young women of color can enhance their beauty. It includes celebrity profiles, health and beauty departments, and fashion sections.

Editorial & Ordering Address:
210 Route 4E
Suite 401
Paramus, NJ 07652
201-843-4004
Orders: 800-403-5791

Audience: M/F, ages 15–19
Subject: Christianity
Circulation: 120,000
Distribution: Sunday schools
Editor: Douglas C. Schmidt
Publisher: David C. Cook Publishing Company
Cost: $1.99/quarter (13 issues)
Sample: Free with SASE

I.D.

is the class-and-home paper for youth-level Sunday school students. Each issue contains a student Bible study for use in class and daily devotions to take home, as well as feature articles related to the day's lesson.

Editorial & Ordering Address:
David C. Cook Publishing Company
4050 Lee Vance View
Colorado Springs, CO 80918
800-426-6596
Fax: 800-430-0726

I Love English

invites you to read for pleasure and to find out about the Anglo-Saxon world with photo reports; stories about England, the United States, Australia; tests; briefs; discussions; pictures of today's stars; and cartoons. Written almost entirely in English, the magazine contains a mini-dictionary so you can understand it all on your own.

Audience: M/F, ages 12–15
Subject: Reports, comics, stars
Circulation: 60,027
Distribution: Homes, news-stands, schools
Editor: Brigitte Roussillon
Publisher: Bayard Presse
Cost: 25 FF/issue; 244 FF/yr.

Editorial Address:
Bayard Presse
3 rue Bayard
Paris 75008, France
331-44-356060
Fax: 331-44-35604

Ordering Address:
Bayard Presse International
BP 12
99505 Paris Entreprise France
331-44-216000

Images Doc

is an indispensable educational aid that helps kids discover for themselves thousands of facts about the past, the present, and the future, with wonderful photos and numerous illustrations of animals, historic subjects, science, different countries, and sports. The texts, concise but full of information, are produced with the help of the top experts in each subject.

Audience: M/F, ages 8–12
Subject: Photos and illustrations about animals, historic subjects, science
Circulation: 86,876
Distribution: Subscriptions, schools, newsstands
Editor: Francoise Récamier
Publisher: Bayard Presse
Cost: 28 FF/issue; 308 FF/yr.

Editorial Address:
Bayard Presse
3 rue Bayard
Paris 75008, France
331-44-356060
Fax: 331-44-35604

Ordering Address:
Bayard Presse International
BP 12
99505 Paris Entreprise France
331-44-216000

In Motion

focuses on developing a safe-driving attitude, maintaining a safe vehicle, and acquiring behind-the-wheel safe-driving skills.

Audience: M/F, high school students
Subject: Driver education
Circulation: 1,000,000
Distribution: Driver's education classes—public and commercial schools
Editor: Carole Rubenstein
Publisher: General Learning Communications
Cost: Free
Sample: Write to editor; include SASE with 78¢ U.S. postage

Editorial & Ordering Address:
General Learning Corporation
900 Skokie Boulevard, Suite 200
Northbrook, IL 60062-4028
847-205-3000
Fax: 847-564-8197

Audience: M/F, ages 12–20
Subject: Art, literature,
photography, music,
cartoons, etc.
Circulation: 25,000
Distribution: Schools (50%);
subscriptions (40%);
newsstands (10%)
Publisher: Jean Baird
Cost: $4.25/issue;
CAN$12.95/yr. (4 issues);
$18.95 U.S. and outside
Canada
Sample: $4.50; write to pub-
lisher
Readers' Work Published:
Poetry, short stories, plays,
computer and fine art,
photography, cartoons

In 2 Print

a national forum for emerging Canadian artists, publishes original works by young adults ages 12–20 including poetry, short stories, plays, painting, photography, computer art, and cartoons. The magazine also publishes an eclectic array of reviews of theater, music, and books. The magazine is committed to creating opportunities and creating an environment that nurtures creative talent and interests.

Editorial & Ordering Address:
P.O. Box 102
Port Colborne, ON
Canada L3K 5I7
905-834-1539
Fax: 905-834-1540
Orders: 888-215-5142

Audience: M/F, ages 7–20
Subject: Shooting sports:
hunting, competitive
shooting
Circulation: 50,000
Distribution: Homes (99%);
schools (1%)
Editor: John E. Robbins
Publisher: National Rifle
Association
Cost: $9.50/school; $15.00 for
youth includes NRA
jr. membership (12 issues)
Sample: Send 9" × 12" SASE
with 75¢ postage
Readers' Work Published:
Occasional articles

InSights Magazine

seeks to promote the safe, responsible, and ethical use of firearms and to interest and educate young people in hunting, marksmanship shooting, conservation, recreational shooting, wildlife, and firearms in general.

Editorial & Ordering Address:
National Rifle Association
11250 Waples Mill Road
Fairfax, VA 22030
703-267-1000
Fax: 703-267-3971

Jack and Jill

is a general interest magazine with an emphasis on health, nutrition, and fitness. Its illustrated stories, articles, poems, and comic strip features are designed to entice young readers while kindling in them an enjoyment of reading. Departments include mazes, and word puzzles.

Audience: M/F, ages 7–10
Subject: General interest, health and fitness
Circulation: 327,000
Distribution: Homes
Editor: Daniel Lee
Publisher: Children's Better Health Institute
Cost: $15.95/yr. (8 issues)
Sample: Teachers and librarians send $1.25 to the editor
Readers' Work Published: Jokes, poetry, stories, drawings, special contests

Editorial Address:
Children's Better Health Institute
1100 Waterway Boulevard
P.O. Box 567
Indianapolis, IN 46206
317-636-8881

Ordering Address:
P.O. Box 10003
Des Moines, IA 50340

J'Aime Lire

is a funny little book that gives kids a taste of reading. *J'aime Lire* encourages young readers between the ages of 7 and 10. Its long illustrated story, its cartoon strip with Tom Tom and Nana characters, and its games are all designed to help beginning readers everywhere to improve their reading.

Audience: M/F, ages 7–10
Subject: Illustrated novel, games, and comics
Circulation: 161,097
Distribution: Homes, newsstands, schools
Editor: Martine Lamy
Publisher: Bayard Presse
Cost: 30 FF/issue; 330 FF/yr.

Editorial Address:
Bayard Presse
3 rue Bayard
Paris 75008, France
331-44-356060
Fax: 331-44-35604

Ordering Address:
Bayard Press International
BP 12
99505 Paris Entreprise France
331-44-216000
Fax: 331-20-274192

Je Bouquine

features a complete novel each month by a modern writer. It also gives information about major works in French or foreign literature through a cartoon strip and a fact file. It also contains a news column and the latest on films, books, television, and songs. It includes a real-life story and competitions with lots of prizes.

Audience: M/F, ages 10–15
Subject: A contemporary novel
Circulation: 65,535
Distribution: Homes, newsstands, schools
Editor: Beatrice Valentin
Publisher: Bayard Presse
Cost: 43 FF/issue; 466 FF/yr.

Editorial Address:
Bayard Presse
3 rue Bayard
Paris 75008, France
331-44-356060
Fax: 331-44-35604

Ordering Address:
Bayard Presse International
BP 12
99505 Paris Entreprise France
331-44-216000
Fax: 331-20-274192

Journal of the West

is published in theme issues with added articles about the West, museum features, and an extensive book review section. The magazine seeks to cover the American West in a broad sense.

Audience: M/F, young adult, adult
Subject: History of the American West
Circulation: 4,500
Distribution: Subscriptions
Editor: Robin Higham
Publisher: Carol A. Williams
Cost: $38.00/yr. individuals; $48.00/yr. instructors (4 issues)
Sample: Free upon request

Editorial & Ordering Address:
Carole A. Williams
1531 Yuma
P.O. Box 1009
Manhattan, KS 66502-4228
913-539-1888
Fax: 913-539-2233

Junior Scholastic

a classroom magazine for students, is designed as a supplement to the classroom social studies curriculum. Issued 18 times during the school year, it features current events, world cultures, U.S. and world history, geography and map-reading lessons, charts, graphs, and reading comprehension activities. This 20-page, 4-color publication has been continuously published for 58 years.

Audience: M/F, grades 6–8
Subject: Social studies
Circulation: 650,000
Distribution: Schools
Editor: Lee Baier
Publisher: Scholastic Inc.
Cost: $6.95/student for 10 or more subscriptions; $11.00/single subscription; $22.00/teacher's edition
Sample: Available to teachers and librarians; contact editor
Readers' Work Published: Letters to the editor, junior reporter news stories

Editorial Address:
Scholastic Inc.
555 Broadway
New York, NY 10012
212-505-3071

Ordering Address:
Scholastic Inc.
2931 E. McCarty Street
P.O. Box 3710
Jefferson City, MO 65102-9957
314-636-8890

Junior Trails

is a religious publication slanted toward preteen boys and girls. Fiction stories seek to present realistic characters working out problems according to biblical principles. Nonfiction articles include a spiritual emphasis, pointing out God's handiwork, care, wisdom, or creativity.

Audience: M/F, ages 10–12
Subject: Bible-based problem solving
Circulation: 45,000
Distribution: Sunday schools
Editor: Sinda S. Zinn
Publisher: Gospel Publishing House
Cost: $8.00/yr. (52 issues)

Editorial & Ordering Address:
Gospel Publishing House
1445 Boonville Avenue
Springfield, MO 65802
417-862-2781

Karate/Kung Fu Illustrated

is dedicated to providing insight into the martial arts. It includes articles on history, personalities, and technique how-to's in the karate and kung fu world. The publication covers both traditional and sport karate.

Editorial & Ordering Address:
Rainbow Publications
P.O. Box 918
Santa Clarita, CA 91380
800-423-2874 or 805-254-4066
Fax: 805-254-3028

Audience: M/F, all ages
Subject: Martial arts
Circulation: 35,000
Distribution: Subscriptions (25%); newsstands (75%)
Editor: Robert W. Young
Publisher: Michael Jones
Cost: $2.95/issue; $9.75/yr. (6 issues)
Sample: Free with 9" × 12" SASE
Readers' Work Published: Articles about children martial artists, styles for children

Keynoter

is the official publication of Key Club International (the world's largest high school service organization, under Kiwanis International). *Keynoter* strives to address topical teen issues through educational, informative, self-help features.

Editorial & Ordering Address:
Key Club International
3636 Woodview Trace
Indianapolis, IN 46268
317-875-8755

Audience: M/F, high school students
Subject: Official publication for Key Club International
Circulation: 4,200 (members)
Distribution: Directly to clubs
Editor: Julie A. Carson
Publisher: Key Club International
Cost: $4.00/yr. (7 issues)
Sample: Send 9" × 12" SASE with 65¢ postage
Readers' Work Published: Teen-related submissions

Keys for Kids

promotes high moral and spiritual values through daily devotional. For each day there is an interesting story from everyday life, based on a biblical principle and followed by a practical application. They are also accompanied by appropriate scripture suggestions.

Editorial & Ordering Address:
Children's Bible Hour
Box 1
Grand Rapids, MI 49501
616-451-2009

Audience: M/F, elementary school ages
Subject: Wide variety—all daily devotionals
Circulation: 40,000
Distribution: Homes (90%); churches (10%)
Editor: Hazel Marett
Publisher: Children's Bible Hour
Cost: Free one to a family upon request

Kid City

Audience: M/F, ages 6–10
Subject: General interest, reading and writing
Distribution: Homes
Editor: Bill Doyle
Publisher: Nina Link
Cost: $13.95/yr.
Readers' Work Published: Letters, poems, inventions, news

seeks to involve readers and to encourage them to interact with the fiction, poetry, articles, puzzles, games, and other activities which appear in the magazine. With themes ranging from space and flight to animals and nature, *Kid City* places an emphasis on engaging readers' interest in reading and writing.

Editorial Address:
Children's Television
 Workshop
One Lincoln Plaza
New York, NY 10023
212-595-3456

Ordering Address:
200 Watt Street
P.O. Box 2924
Boulder, CO 80322

Kids Discover

Audience: M/F, ages 6–12
Subject: Each issue addresses a single subject (weather, Colonial America)
Circulation: 400,000
Distribution: Homes (85%); libraries, doctors (15%)
Editor: Stella Sands
Publisher: Mark Levine
Cost: $3.00/issue; $19.95/yr. (10 issues)
Sample: $3.00

seeks to stimulate children's curiosity and desire to learn by presenting information about fascinating subjects in a fun-to-read and easy-to-grasp format. Kid friendly, it's a vehicle for kids to explore all aspects of the world around them. Each issue is filled with a wealth of information about a single subject.

Editorial & Ordering Address:
170 Fifth Avenue, 6th Floor
New York, NY 10010
212-242-5133
Fax: 212-242-5628

KSE News (Kids for Saving Earth News)

Audience: M/F, ages 7–13
Subject: Environmental issues
Circulation: 300,000
Distribution: Homes, schools (5%); retail, other (95%)
Editor: Cynthia Dilliard
Publisher: Kids for Saving Earth
Cost: As part of KSE membership, $15.00/club (4 issues)
Sample: Write to P.O. Box given
Readers' Work Published: Artwork, letters, poetry

The mission of Kids for Saving Earth is to educate, empower, and inspire kids of all ages to unite to take peaceful action on behalf of the environment. KSE, the sponsoring organization, supports the local community efforts of kids through its educational programs and by networking with other organizations.

Editorial & Ordering Address:
Kids for Saving Earth
P.O. Box 47247
Plymouth, MN 55447
612-525-0002
Fax: 612-525-0243

Audience: M/F, ages 8–14
Subject: Various themes
Circulation: 2.5 million
Distribution: Inserted in 40 daily newspapers (U.S., Guam, Virgin Islands)
Editor: Anita Sama
Publisher: Gannett Co. Inc.
Readers' Work Published: Letters, poems, jokes, recipes

Kids Today

is a national newspaper supplement for young readers established to help stir children's interest in reading the newspaper. It uses news, entertainment, sports, and feature stories in its 4-page tab and 1-page broadcast format. There are also puzzles and weekly columns for reader participation.

Editorial & Ordering Address:
1000 Wilson Boulevard
Arlington, VA 22229-0002
703-276-3780

Audience: M/F, ages 7–11
Subject: General interest (no violence)
Circulation: 15,000
Distribution: Free to schools; mail to individual for contribution
Editor: Don DiMarco
Publisher: Today Publishing, Inc.
Cost: $5.00 contribution/yr. (3 issues)
Sample: $1.00 to Today Publishing
Readers' Work Published: Poems, short stories, essays, letters, jokes, puzzles

Kids Today Mini-Magazine

seeks to recognize and celebrate imagination, creativity, distinctiveness, and worth of all people, with particular emphasis on all children. Its goal is to stimulate within its young readership an interest and appreciation for the ability to communicate, learn, and entertain through reading, writing, and artistic skills.

Editorial & Ordering Address:
Today Publishing
2724 College Park Road
Allison Park, PA 15101
412-486-1564

Audience: M/F, grades K–6
Subject: Animal/environmental protection
Circulation: 1 million+
Distribution: Schools
Editor: Bill DeRosa
Publisher: National Association for Humane & Environmental Education
Cost: $20.00/school yr. (9 issues)
Sample: Contact Circulation Dept.
Readers' Work Published: Letters, accounts of animals, environmental activities

KIND News (Kids In Nature's Defense)

is the award-winning classroom newspaper that teaches students the importance of kindness and respect toward people, animals, and the Earth. Articles, puzzles, and activities span the elementary-school curriculum and help children discover the joy of reading.

Editorial & Ordering Address:
P.O. Box 362
East Haddam, CT 06423-0362
860-434-8666
Fax: 860-434-9579
Fax Orders: 860-434-6282

Know Your World Extra

Audience: M/F, grades 6–10
Subject: Social studies for special education
Distribution: Schools
Editor: Scott Ingram
Publisher: Richard J. LeBrasseur
Cost: $8.45 /subscription for 10 or more sets
Sample: Contact customer service

is a 12-page special education periodical. The reading level never exceeds 3.0. It presents a wide variety of high-interest topics to students with their interests and abilities in mind. The publication features news, science, narratives, survival skills, and games.

Editorial Address:
Weekly Reader Corp.
P.O. Box 2791
Middletown, CT 06457-9291
203-638-2400
Fax: 203-246-5964

Ordering Address:
Weekly Reader Corp.
3001 Cindel Drive
Delran, NJ 08370
800-446-3355

Koala Club News

Audience: M/F, ages 15 and under
Subject: Animals
Circulation: 100,000
Editor: Georgeanne Irvine
Publisher: Zoological Society of San Diego
Cost: $12.00/member (6 issues)
Sample: Write to San Diego Zoo Public Relations
Readers' Work Published: Letters, original poems, drawings, stories

is a magazine about animals. The 8-page bimonthly magazine goes to kids who are members of the Zoological Society of San Diego Koala Club. It focuses on news about animals, the Zoo and Wild Animal Park, plants, and conservation. It includes articles, photos, and a coloring page.

Editorial Address:
Zoological Society of San Diego
P.O. Box 551
San Diego, CA 92112
619-231-1515

Ordering Address:
San Diego Zoo
Membership Department
P.O. Box 271
San Diego, CA 92112
619-231-1515

Kol ha'T'nua

Audience: M/F, grades 8–12
Subject: Jewish topics and Israel
Circulation: 1,800
Distribution: Subscriptions
Editor: Daniel Malino
Publisher: Young Judaea
Cost: $18.00/yr.
Sample: Write to Young Judaea office
Readers' Work Published: Articles written by members of Young Judaea

is an expression of Young Judaea, the Zionist youth movement sponsored by Hadassah. The quarterly newspaper attempts to educate and inform teenagers on a range of Jewish topics. It is a forum and communication network for the 1,800 high school members of the movement to express opinions concerning Young Judaea, Zionism, Judaism, America, Israel, youth, and current events.

Editorial & Ordering Address:
50 W. 58th Street
New York, NY 10019
212-247-9210
Fax: 212-247-9240

Koululainen

Audience: M/F, ages 7–12
Subject: General interest
Circulation: 45,054
Editor: Sirkku Kuusava
Publisher: Yhtyneet Kuvalehdet Oy
Cost: FIM 220 plus postage
Readers' Work Published: Stories

seeks to be an adventure specially for girls and boys. It contains a good dose of humor, warmth, and security, as well as of fact and fantasy. The magazine has stories about animals, hobbies, and pastimes. It has exciting puzzles, cartoons, and pictures of music and sports idols. It also offers readers the chance to have stories published.

Editorial & Ordering Address:
Yhtyneet Kuvalehdet Oy
Postilokero 150
Maistraatinportti 1
00240 Helsinki, Finland
358-0-1566 524
Fax: 358-0-1566 505

La Giostra (The Merry Go Round)

Audience: M/F, ages 3–7
Subject: Tales, nursery rhymes, games, artworking, religion
Circulation: 50,000
Distribution: Homes (50%); schools (50%)
Editor: Domenico Volpi
Publisher: A.V.E.
Cost: LIT 20,000/yr.
Sample: Free
Readers' Work Published: Letters, pictures

seeks to stimulate a dialogue between adults and kids. Every issue includes literary and art arguments fit to childhood. It includes tales, real life, nursery rhymes, games, and jokes to improve children's educational and social skills, while providing a Christian education. This 32-page, 4-color monthly (except July and August) first appeared in 1969.

Editorial & Ordering Address:
A.V.E. (Anonima Veritas Editrice) S.r.l.
Via Aurelia, 481
Rome 00165, Italy
Fax: 662-0207

Lad

Audience: M, grades 1–3
Subject: Southern Baptist missions education
Circulation: 61,000
Distribution: Churches
Editor: Charlotte Teas
Publisher: Brotherhood Commission
Cost: $3.09/quarter (12 issues yr.)
Sample: Include SASE
Readers' Work Published: Art, news, jokes

is published for boys who are members of the Southern Baptist Royal Ambassador program. The main task of the program is to help boys know about missions and how they can have a personal role in missions.

Editorial & Ordering Address:
Brotherhood Commission, SBC
1548 Poplar Avenue
Memphis, TN 38104
901-272-2461
Fax: 901-726-5540

Audience: M/F, ages 2–6
Subject: General interest
Circulation: 130,000
Distribution: Homes, schools, libraries, bookstores
Editor: Marianne Carus
Publisher: Robert Harper
Cost: $32.97 (12 issues)
Sample: $4.00 to LADYBUG Sample Copy, P.O. Box 300, Peru, IL 61354

Ladybug, The Magazine for Young Children

is a collection of the best stories, poems, songs, games, and adventures for young children. Each page is beautifully illustrated and guaranteed to delight parents and children alike.

Editorial Address:
Carus Publishing
315 Fifth Street
Peru, IL 61354
815-224-6656

Ordering Address:
P.O. Box 7436
Red Oak, IA 51591-4486
800-827-0227

Audience: M/F, ages 3–6
Subject: School readiness skills
Distribution: Homes, daycare centers
Editor: Sumiyo Nagata
Publisher: Fukutake Publishing Company

Learningland

is a multimedia program that provides the opportunity and material for a unique at-home, interactive preschool learning experience. The product materials include a picture book, activity book, audio cassette, parent newsletter, *Learning Together*, and a Fun Kit which contains various hands-on crafts all coordinated to a single theme.

Editorial & Ordering Address:
Challenge Plus Workshop
3838 Carson Street, Suite 200
Torrance, CA 90503
310-540-4988
Fax: 310-316-4412

Audience: M/F, young adult, adult
Subject: Internationally serves needs of left-handed people
Distribution: Subscriptions (100%)
Editor: Suzan Ireland

Lefthander Magazine

seeks to promote the needs and interests of left-handers by publishing the latest left-handedness research, offering advice and tips to children and parents about writing, tying shoes, and learning methods, and by entertaining and educating the public.

Editorial & Ordering Address:
P.O. Box 8249
Topeka, KS 66608

Audience: M/F, ages 3–7
Subject: Stories and games
Circulation: 67,901
Distribution: Homes, schools, newsstands
Editor: Marie Agnés Gaudrat Pourcel
Publisher: Bayard Presse
Cost: 35 FF/issue; 385 FF/yr.

Les Belles Histoires (Beautiful Stories)

is the number one collection of stories for children. Every month, the best writers and illustrators of children's books introduce beginning readers to the pleasure of books and stories. This is a good source of stories for parents to share with their children.

Editorial Address:
Bayard Presse
3 rue Bayard
Paris 75008, France
331-44-356060
Fax: 331-44-35604

Ordering Address:
Bayard Presse International
BP 12
99505 Paris Entreprise France
331-44-216000
Fax: 331-20-274192

Let's Find Out

Audience: M/F, preK–kindergarten
Subject: Science, social studies–theme centered
Editor: Mary Reid
Publisher: Scholastic Inc.
Cost: $4.95/subscription for 10 or more subscriptions; available in Spanish
Sample: Free on request

is designed as a classroom resource to introduce pre-school and kindergarten children to the world around them. Presented in 8 theme-centered monthly issues including two-sided posters and "Discovery Cards" as well as teachers' materials and a parent letter, this 4-color magazine includes a variety of illustrations and photos.

Editorial Address:
Scholastic Inc.
555 Broadway
New York, NY 10012

Ordering Address:
Scholastic Inc.
2931 E. McCarty Street
P.O. Box 3710
Jefferson City, MO 65102-9957
800-651-1586

Literary Cavalcade

Audience: M/F, high school students and teachers
Subject: Contemporary literature and authors
Circulation: 200,000
Distribution: Schools
Editor: Cynthia Sosland Summers
Publisher: Scholastic Inc.
Cost: $7.95/subscription (8 issues)
Sample: Contact ordering address
Readers' Work Published: Student writing

seeks to publish the finest in contemporary literature for senior high school English classes. Each issue features a variety of writing that includes major literary authors, modern classics, excerpts from bestsellers, top-quality drama and film scripts, and poetry, as well as a "Writer's Workshop" and features designed to help students prepare for college entrance examinations.

Editorial Address:
Scholastic Inc.
555 Broadway
New York, NY 10012
212-343-6423
Fax: 212-343-6333
E-mail: literary@scholastic.com

Ordering Address:
Scholastic Inc.
2931 E. McCarty Street
P.O. Box 3710
Jefferson City, MO 65102-9957
800-325-6149

The Magazine for Christian Youth!

Audience: M/F, ages 11–18
Subject: Christian teens' growth helps, humor
Circulation: 35,000
Distribution: Churches, homes, schools
Editor: Anthony E. Peterson
Publisher: United Methodist Publishing House
Cost: $2.00/issue; $18.00/yr. (12 issues)
Sample: Request from Kathy Hagy at editorial address
Readers' Work Published: Letters, stories, articles, poetry

seeks to help teenagers develop Christian identity and live the Christian faith in their contemporary culture.

Editorial Address:
201 Eighth Avenue S.
P.O. Box 801
Nashville, TN 37202-0801
615-749-6015
Fax: 615-749-6074

Ordering Address:
Cokesbury Subscriptions
P.O. Box 801
Nashville, TN 37202-0801

Audience: M/F, ages 10–17
Subject: Environmental education
Distribution: Club members
Editor: Peter Ottaru
Publisher: Malihai Clubs of Tanzania

Malihai Clubs Newsletter

serves members of Malihai Clubs of Tanzania, an organization for conservation education. It seeks to serve as a forum to educate the youth of Tanzania about the environment; to increase the awareness and understanding of economic, scientific, and aesthetic values of natural resources; and to promote the spirit of conservation and wise use of the land.

Editorial & Ordering Address:
Malihai Clubs of Tanzania
P.O. Box 1541
Arusha, Tanzania
057-6026

Audience: M/F, grades 6–9
Subject: Fiction and artwork by teens
Circulation: 25,000
Distribution: Schools (60%); newsstands (20%); homes (20%)
Editor: R. James Stahl
Publisher: R. James Stahl
Cost: $21.95/yr.(4 issues); $7.25/subscription for 10+ subscriptions to one school
Sample: Free catalog available by written request or calling toll-free number
Readers' Work Published: Stories, poems, plays, letters, essays, reviews

Merlyn's Pen: The National Magazine of Student Writing, Grades 6–9

publishes fiction and expository writing by teens in the United States. The 150 pieces it prints each year are selected from some 15,000 manuscripts. *Merlyn's Pen* editors respond personally to every teen contributor and sometimes guide students through the revision process. Here's an opportunity for teens to read the best work by their peers.

Editorial & Ordering Address:
Merlyn's Pen, Inc.
4 King Street
P.O. Box 910
East Greenwich, RI 02818
401-885-5175 or 800-247-2027
Fax: 401-885-5222
E-mail: merlynspen@aol.com

Audience: M/F, grades 9–12
Subject: Fiction and artwork by teens
Circulation: 15,000
Distribution: Schools (60%); newsstands (10%); homes (30%)
Editor: R. James Stahl
Publisher: R. James Stahl
Cost: $21.95/yr.(4 issues); $7.25/subscription for 10+ subscriptions to one school
Sample: Free catalog available by written request or calling toll-free number
Readers' Work Published: Stories, poems, plays, letters, essays, reviews

Merlyn's Pen Senior Edition: Grades 9–12

is designed for teenagers in search of good reading. All of the fiction appearing here—the stories, poems, letters, plays, and essays—is written by teens in grades 9–12. Every contributor receives a written response from an editor within 10 weeks. Here's a chance for teen readers to see the best work by their peers.

Editorial & Ordering Address:
Merlyn's Pen, Inc.
4 King Street
P.O. Box 910
East Greenwich, RI 02818
401-885-5175 or 800-247-2027
Fax: 401-885-5222
E-mail: merlynspen@aol.com

MetroKids Magazine

provides information about the Philadelphia region for local and visiting families. Kids write the restaurant reviews; other columns include reviews of books, videos, and software. Features cover parents' concerns and ways these can be handled locally. The Never-a-Dull-Moment calendar gives a day-by-day listing of events and activities for kids and families.

Audience: M/F, children under 13 years and parents
Subject: Resources, information, and activities; games and software for families in greater Delaware Valley
Circulation: 75,000
Distribution: Schools (30%); retail outlets (50%)
Editor: Nancy Lisagor
Publisher: KidStuff Publications, Inc.
Cost: Single copy free; $18.00/yr. (12 issues)
Sample: Send $2.00
Readers' Work Published: A kids' column each month

Editorial & Ordering Address:
KidStuff Publications, Inc.
1080 N. Delaware Avenue
Suite 702
Philadelphia, PA 19112
215-291-5560
Fax: 215-291-5563
E-mail: metrokids@family.com

The Mini Page

a 4-page educational tabloid for kids from K–12, appears in over 450 newspapers and is often a part of Newspaper in Education (NIE) programs. Each issue centers around a special theme with editorial copy and related puzzles and activities. Available through newspapers.

Audience: M/F, ages 5–12
Subject: General interest
Distribution: Homes, schools
Editor: Betty Debnam
Publisher: Betty Debnam
Sample: Contact Universal Press Syndicate

Editorial Address:
P.O. Box 70567
Washington, DC 20024
202-488-7919

Ordering Address:
Universal Press Syndicate
P.O. Box 419150
Kansas City, MO 64141
816-932-6600

Model Railroader

has been helping hobbyists since 1934 with practical, easy-to-follow, and authoritative advice on how to design and build their own layouts. From prototype drawings and track plans to electricity and electronics, it covers the "nuts and bolts" hobbyists need to know about, while inspiring them with colorful photos and tours of some of the world's greatest layouts. *Model Railroader* covers all scales and eras and provides pure pleasure for modelers of all skill levels.

Audience: M/F, ages 9 years–adult
Subject: Model/real railroading
Distribution: Subscriptions (65%); newsstands (35%)
Editor: Andy Sperandeo, Managing Editor
Publisher: Kalmbach Publishing Co.
Cost: $28.95/year; Canada add $6 for postage; other countries add $11 postage

Editorial & Ordering Address:
21027 Crossroads Circle
P.O. Box 1612
Waukesha, WI 53187
414-796-8776
Fax: 414-796-0126
Orders: 800-553-6644

Audience: M/F, ages 8–14
Subject: History and geography of a different state in each issue; up to date information in health and science
Distribution: Homes, schools
Editor: Phyllis B. Goldman
Publisher: North Carolina Learning Institute for Fitness & Education
Cost: Monkeyshines on America $22.95/yr. (5 issues)

Monkeyshines

is a reading resource for elementary, middle, junior high, and high school students and their teachers. Publications include two periodicals, *Monkeyshines on America* and *Monkeyshines on Health and Science*. They focus on history, geography, and the health sciences. *Monkeyshines* publications also include an ongoing list of new books encompassing a variety of topics ranging from history, geography, and science to trivia and humor.

Editorial & Ordering Address:
North Carolina Learning Institute for Fitness & Education
P.O. Box 10245
Greensboro, NC 27404
910-292-6999
Fax: 910-292-6999
E-mail: mkshines@aol.com

Audience: M/F, ages 6–12
Subject: Religion— Catholic-focused articles
Circulation: 13,000
Distribution: Individual subscriptions, church rack displays
Editor: Sister Kathryn James Hermes
Publisher: St. Paul Books and Media, Daughters of St. Paul
Cost: $2.00/issue; $18.00/yr. (10 issues)
Sample: 9" × 12" SASE with 4 U.S. 1st class stamps
Readers' Work Published: Art, poetry

My Friend: The Catholic Magazine for Kids

offers 32 pages of inspiration, information, and fun for kids at home and in religion class. Bible stories and lives of saints are only the beginning. *My Friend* brings children into contact with God's world and the Church's liturgy and life through crafts, puzzles, fiction stories, nonfiction articles, devotions, and copier material.

Editorial & Ordering Address:
St. Paul Books and Media
50 St. Paul's Avenue
Jamaica Plain
Boston, MA 02130
617-522-8911
Fax: 617-524-8035
Orders: 800-876-4463

Audience: M/F, ages 8–17
Subject: Culture, tradition, values
Circulation: 250,000
Distribution: Homes, schools, newsstands
Editor: Jai Prakash Bharti
Publisher: The Hindustan Times Ltd.
Cost: $6.00/issue; $65.00/yr.
Sample: Send letter to the editor (sample is free)
Readers' Work Published: Fiction, poems, and paintings

Nandan

is the largest selling children's magazine of India. Many readers worldwide also subscribe. The magazine portrays a vivid panorama of Indian culture, tradition, and values through story telling, poems, and regular features. The magazine touches on ancient sources and also tells its readers about the contemporary world.

Editorial & Ordering Address:
The Hindustan Times Ltd.
18–20 K.G. Street
New Delhi, India
331-8201
Fax: 331-9062

National Geographic World

Audience: M/F, ages 8–14
Subject: Natural history, science, outdoor adventure
Circulation: 1.1 million
Distribution: Homes (94%); libraries (6%)
Editor: Susan Mondshein Tejada
Publisher: National Geographic Society
Cost: $2.50/issue; $17.95/yr. (12 issues)
Sample: Free on request
Readers' Work Published: Artwork, letters

aims to inspire in junior members curiosity about their world and beyond, to encourage geographic awareness, and to provide access to the benefits of membership in and resources of the National Geographic Society. Children who subscribe to *World* become junior members of the National Geographic Society.

Editorial Address:
National Geographic
1145 17th Street NW
Washington, DC 20036
202-857-7000
Fax: 202-429-5712

Ordering Address:
National Geographic
P.O. Box 2330
Washington, DC 20013-2330
800-638-4077; 800-548-9797

New Era Magazine

Audience: M/F, ages 12–18
Subject: Youth and religion; L.D.S. (Mormon) lifestyle; general interest
Circulation: 200,000
Distribution: Subscriptions
Editor: Richard M. Romney
Publisher: The Church of Jesus Christ of Latter-day Saints
Cost: $1.00/issue; $8.00/yr. (12 issues)
Sample: $1.00 and a 9" × 12" SASE
Readers' Work Published: Personal experiences, fiction, poetry, letters

established in 1971 for young people of the Church of Jesus Christ of Latter-day Saints, church leaders, and teachers, publishes nonfiction showing how the Church of Jesus Christ of Latter-day Saints is relevant in the lives of young people today. There is special interest in the experience of young Mormons in other countries and stories about successful family relationships.

Editorial & Ordering Address:
The Church of Jesus Christ of Latter-day Saints
50 E. North Temple Street, Floor 23
Salt Lake City, UT 84150
801-240-2951
Fax: 801-240-1727
Orders: 801-240-2947

New Moon: The Magazine for Girls and Their Dreams

Audience: F, ages 8–14
Subject: Dreams, stories, poems, drawings, opinions, reviews, questions, theme ideas
Circulation: 25,000
Editor: Barbara Stretchberry and Tya Ward
Publishers: Joe Kelly, Nancy Gruver
Cost: $25.00/yr. (6 issues)
Sample: $6.50

is a 48-page, advertising free, award winning international magazine with stories by and about girls and women all over the world. *New Moon* celebrates girls, explores the passage from girl to woman, and builds resilience and healthy resistance to the gender inequities girls experience. *New Moon* is for every girl who wants her voice heard and dreams taken seriously.

Editorial Address:
P.O. Box 3620
Duluth, MN 55806
218-728-5507
Fax: 218-728-1812
E-mail: newmoon@newmoon.duluth.mn.us

Ordering Address:
P.O. Box 3587
Duluth, MN 55803-3587
218-728-5507

Nickelodeon Magazine

Audience: M/F, ages 6–14
Subject: Humor
Circulation: 600,000
Distribution: Newsstands (25%); subscriptions (75%)
Editor: Laura Galen
Cost: $2.95/issue; $17.97/yr. (10 issues)
Readers' Work Published: Letters, contests

is a humor magazine for kids ages 6–14. Its original content is both informative and entertaining. The magazine engages readers with its wit, attitude, and interactive features. *Nickelodeon* translates the sensibility and energy of the network into print, so kids can take it wherever they go.

Editorial Address:
1515 Broadway, 41st Floor
New York, NY 10036
212-258-7388
Fax: 212-846-1766
E-mail: nickeditor@aol.com

Ordering Address:
P.O. Box 0945
Des Moines, IA 50340-0945
515-280-8750

Nineteenth Avenue

Audience: M/F, grades 6–10
Subject: Current affairs, arts and humanities
Circulation: 10,000
Distribution: Schools, subscriptions
Editor: Ann Kjelsberg
Publisher: Stephen Sandell, The Humphrey Forum
Cost: $12.00/yr. (6 issues); $40.00/classroom subscription (30 copies/6 issues)
Sample: Call or write
Readers' Work Published: Essays, letters, fiction

encourages students to recognize their important role in public affairs; practice skills of reading, writing, and discussion; develop the habit of using a newspaper; and respect the variety of ideas, opinion, and information in a pluralistic world.

Editorial & Ordering Address:
The Humphrey Forum
301-19th Avenue S.
Minneapolis, MN 55455
612-624-5893
Fax: 612-625-6351

Nipitiri

Audience: M/F, ages 6–12
Subject: General interest
Circulation: 5,000
Distribution: Homes (40%); schools (40%); newsstands (20%)
Editor: Alo Soolo
Publisher: Oliver Leif
Cost: $2.00/issue; $20.00/yr.
Sample: Contact editor, sample is free
Readers' Work Published: All kinds

published in Estonia, seeks to stimulate creative and intellectual abilities of kids ages 6–12. Based on the belief that challenge stimulates learning, *Nipitiri* attempts to encourage mental activities of kids by publishing stories, games, puzzles, short novels, and children's own works. The 32-page, 4-color and black and white monthly first appeared in 1994.

Editorial & Ordering Address:
Vaimukirjastuse as
Narua Mnt 11A – Pk 7
Tallinn EE0001 Estonia
372-6-466284
Fax: 372-6-408399
E-mail: vaim@zen.estpak.ee

Norsk Barneblad

seeks to give children something to read in Nynorsk, a minority language in Norway. The magazine first appeared in 1887.

Audience: M/F, ages 7–15
Subject: General interest
Circulation: 6,000
Distribution: Subscriptions
Editor: Gard Espeland
Publisher: Norsk Barneblad
Cost: NOK 308/yr. (22 issues)
Sample: Free—write or fax
Readers' Work Published:
Letters, stories, voices

Editorial & Ordering Address:
Norsk Barneblad
0180 Oslo, Norway
47-22-425280
Fax: 47-22-425284

Odyssey

Each theme-related 48-page issue is made up of full-length articles, a star chart and observation activity, a current events section devoted to space, a look at other scientific disciplines, and accounts of what is happening at the local and U.S. national levels. *Odyssey's* appeal grows from its effort to generate extensive reader involvement.

Audience: M/F, ages 8–14
Subject: Space exploration
and astronomy
Circulation: 27,000
Distribution: Schools, homes
Editor: Elizabeth Lindstrom
Publisher: Lyell C. Dawes,
Cobblestone Publishing, Inc.
Cost: $24.95/yr. (9 issues)
Sample: $5.70 with request to
editorial address
Readers' Work Published:
Letters, art, poems, contest
entries

Editorial & Ordering Address:
Cobblestone Publishing, Inc.
7 School Street
Peterborough, NH 03458
603-924-7209
Fax: 603-924-7380

Okapi

has files to collect and keep. It contains in-depth reports to read and dream about and offers practical advice, tests and features on health, the environment, and careers. It also features the "Tabloid," an 8-page color newspaper about the hobbies and pastimes of 10- to 15-year olds as well as the big news stories from around the world.

Audience: M/F, ages 10–15
Subject: In-depth report on
health, environment, and
careers
Circulation: 95,000
Distribution: Subscriptions,
schools, newsstands
Editor: Sylvaine de Paulin,
Martine de Sauto
Publisher: Bayard Presse
Cost: 28 FF/issue; 515 FF/yr.

Editorial Address:
Bayard Presse
3 rue Bayard
Paris 75008, France
331-44-356060
Fax: 331-44-35604

Ordering Address:
Bayard Presse International
BP 12
99505 Paris Entreprise France
331-44-216000

Olomeinu/Our World

Audience: M/F, elementary school students
Subject: Material of Jewish religious interest
Circulation: 18,000
Distribution: Schools (90%); homes (10%)
Editor: Rabbi Yaakov Fruchter and Rabbi Nosson Scherman
Publisher: Torah Umesorah– National Society for Hebrew Day Schools
Cost: $8.00/bulk; $10.00/ individual (8 issues)
Readers' Work Published: Letters, poems, short stories, contest entries

is a publication for children attending Jewish all-day schools/Yeshivas or afternoon Hebrew schools. It contains religious material dealing with Jewish laws and customs, holidays, the Torah, history, and current events. The material is in the form of short stories, poems, special features, etc., intended to stimulate an interest in the above.

Editorial & Ordering Address:
Torah Umesorah—National Society for Hebrew Day Schools
5723–18th Avenue
Brooklyn, NY 11204-1932
718-259-1223
Fax: 718-259-1795

On the Line

Audience: M/F, ages 10–14
Subject: Leisure reading, puzzles, activities
Circulation: 9,000
Distribution: Churches (85%); homes (15%)
Editor: Mary Clemens Meyer
Publisher: Mennonite Publishing House/Faith and Life Press
Cost: $18.90/yr. (12 issues)
Sample: Send a 7" × 9" SASE
Readers' Work Published: Letters, poetry, short stories

seeks to help children understand and appreciate God, the created world, themselves, and others. Stories and articles offer readers help in feeling like persons of worth, handling problems, accepting diverse races and cultures, nurturing a desire for world peace, and reinforcing Christian values.

Editorial Address:
Mennonite Publishing House
616 Walnut Avenue
Scottdale, PA 15683
412-887-8500
Fax: 412-887-3111

Ordering Address:
Faith and Life Press
P.O. Box 347
Newton, KS 67114-0347
316-283-5100
Fax: 316-283-0454

Otterwise: For Kids Who Are into Saving Animals & the Environment

Audience: M/F, ages 8–13
Subject: Animal welfare, environment
Circulation: 3,000
Distribution: Homes (33%); schools (50%); newsstands (17%)
Editor: Cheryl Miller
Publisher: Otterwise, Inc.
Cost: $8.00/yr.
Sample: $2.00
Readers' Work Published: Stories, art, poems, letters

a newsletter for ages 8–13, is for kids who love animals. Through informative articles, lively stories, and entertaining activities and puzzles, the newsletter helps develop children's compassion for animals and the natural world around them.

Editorial & Ordering Address:
P.O. Box 1374
Portland, ME 04104
207-283-2964

Owl: The Discovery Magazine for Kids

has entertained and educated kids for over 20 years. Each 32-page issue is filled with fascinating stories, mind-bending games and puzzles, a pull-out poster, the popular Mighty Mites comic strip, and a Dr. Zed science experiment.

Audience: M/F, ages 8 and up
Subject: Nature, science, animals, and technology
Circulation: 110,000 U.S. and Canada
Distribution: Subscriptions (98%); other (2%)
Editor: Nyla Ahmad
Publisher: Owl Communications
Cost: CAN$20.33/GST included; $21.00/yr. U.S. (10 issues)
Sample: Free upon request
Readers' Work Published: Drawings, letters, stories, poetry

Editorial Address:
Young Naturalist Foundation
179 John Street
Suite 500
Toronto, ON
Canada M5T 3G5
416-971-5275
Fax: 416-971-5294
E-mail: owlcom@owl.on.ca

Ordering Address:
In U.S.:
25 Boxwood Lane
Buffalo, NY 14227-2780

Partha

aims to help and guide children and teens into adult life.

Audience: M/F, ages 13–18
Subject: Success, self-development, careers, health
Circulation: 4,600
Distribution: Subscriptions only
Editor: Anant Pai
Publisher: Anant Pai
Cost: $4.00/issue; $45.00/yr.
Sample: Free sample copy to schools

Editorial & Ordering Address:
Partha Institute of Personality Development
409 Laxmi Commercial Centre
S.B. Road
Dadar (W) Bombay 400028, India
422-3494

Phosphore

is published in France to help you through your lycee years successfully, from third year to your final year. Each issue includes news and historical fact files, pull-out specials on all the subjects, advice about which path to choose, and about ways of studying. *Phosphore* also offers a clear and detailed look at economics, science, international affairs, and culture in the modern world.

Audience: M/F, ages 14–20
Subject: News and historical fact files; advice about ways of studying
Circulation: 103,654
Distribution: Homes, newsstands, schools
Editor: Jean Jacques Fresco
Publisher: Bayard Presse
Cost: 35 FF/issue; 398 FF/yr.

Editorial Address:
Bayard Presse
3 rue Bayard
Paris 75008, France
331-44-356060
Fax: 331-44-35604

Ordering Address:
Bayard Presse International
BP 12
99505 Paris Entreprise France
331-44-216000

Audience: M/F, ages 6–17
Subject: Dramatic material, especially for celebration of holidays and special occasions
Circulation: 11,000
Distribution: Schools, libraries, drama clubs, community theaters
Editor: Elizabeth Preston
Publisher: Sylvia K. Burack
Cost: $28.00/yr. (7 issues); $52.00/2 yrs.
Sample: Send request and $3.50

Plays, The Drama Magazine for Young People

is a complete source of original, royalty-free plays and programs for school-age actors and audiences. Each issue includes 8–10 plays arranged by age level, including modern and traditional plays for the celebration of all important holidays and special occasions as well as skits, comedies, dramas, mysteries, fairy tales, folktales, and puppet plays.

Editorial & Ordering Address:
Plays, Inc.
120 Boylston Street
Boston, MA 02116-4615
617-423-3157
Fax: 617-423-2168

Audience: M/F, ages 6–12
Subject: Religion
Circulation: 102,000
Distribution: Homes (33%); churches (66%)
Editor: Janet R. Knight
Publisher: The Upper Room
Cost: $16.95/yr. (11 issues)
Sample: 7" × 9" SASE with $1.10 U.S. postage
Readers' Work Published: Letters, poems, stories, art

Pockets

is a devotional magazine for children to help them understand the Christian tradition through fiction, poetry, scripture, prayer, and activities. *Pockets* explains Jesus' life and teachings to children. Designed for children of many ethnic backgrounds, *Pockets* addresses a wide variety of concerns and needs.

Editorial Address:
The Upper Room
1908 Grand Avenue
Box 189
Nashville, TN 37202-0189
615-340-7333
Fax: 615-340-7006
E-mail: 102615.3127@compuserve.com

Ordering Address:
Pockets
P.O. Box 37 146
Boone, IA 50037-0146
800-925-6847

Audience: Children
Subject: World of catechism— communication of faith
Circulation: 42,000
Distribution: Subscriptions, schools, newsstands
Editor: Muriel De Souich
Publisher: Bayard Presse
Cost: 33 FF/issue; 159 FF/yr.

Points De Repére

offers different subjects to think about, helpful advice to put to use in your catechism, information about the lives and psychology of children, and essential references for the communication of faith. Produced in association with the National Center for Religious Education.

Editorial Address:
Bayard Presse
3 rue Bayard
Paris 75008, France
331-44-356060
Fax: 331-44-35604

Ordering Address:
Bayard Presse International
BP 12
99505 Paris Entreprise France
331-44-216000

Audience: M/F, ages 3–7
Subject: Illustrated stories,
*   games, humorous, inge-*
*   nious, informative features*
Circulation: 114,430
Distribution: Subscriptions,
*   schools, newsstands*
Editor: Maire-Agnés Gaudrat
Publisher: Bayard Presse
Cost: 29 FF/issue; 299 FF/yr.

Pomme D'Api

is the number one magazine for children in Europe. The whole world of childhood can be found in *Pomme D'Api*: exciting characters, beautifully illustrated stories, games, and humorous, ingenious, and informative features that give the child instant access to the world. Every month there's a surprise in the middle: a castle, a farm, or a school. A supplement for parents is included, full of practical advice, ideas, and helpful suggestions.

Editorial Address: Ordering Address:
Bayard Presse   Bayard Presse International
3 rue Bayard   BP 12
Paris 75008, France   99505 Paris Entreprise France
331-44-356060   331-44-216000
Fax: 331-44-35604

Audience: M/F, ages 1–3
Subject: Stories
Circulation: 73,554
Distribution: Homes, news-
*   stands, schools*
Editor: Marie Agnés Gaudrat
Publisher: Bayard Presse
Cost: 29 FF/issue; 285 FF/yr.

Popi

is the magazine for tiny tots. Every month in *Popi*, they find a new story about Leo and his monkey Popi, and meet their old friend the Little Brown Bear (who's also on television). With a little surprise to cut out, photos of Popi the monkey and the picture circle, they take their first steps in learning. A real helping hand in the educational awakening of its "little readers," Popi helps guide them from the first words to their first conversations.

Editorial Address: Ordering Address:
Bayard Presse   Bayard Presse International
3 rue Bayard   BP 12
Paris 75008, France   99505 Paris Entreprise France
331-44-356060   331-44-216000
Fax: 331-44-35604   Fax: 331-20-274192

Audience: M/F, advanced
placement high school
students
Subject: Mathematics, science
(primarily physics)
Circulation: 9,000
Distribution: Homes (50%);
schools (50%)
Editor: Timothy Weber
Publisher: Bill G. Aldridge,
National Science Teachers
Association (Springer-
Verlag, copublisher)
Cost: $18.00/yr. (individual);
$14.00/yr. (student);
$30.00/yr. (library/institu-
tion); bulk rate for
classes available; $5.00/
single and back issues
Sample: Available from
ordering address

Quantum

is the English-language version of the Russian journal *Kvant* and contains translated as well as original material. It seeks to explore everyday phenomena, classic findings, and out-of-the-way corners of math and science. *Quantum* engages its readers with interspersed questions and problems to induce the joy of discovery and the satisfaction of meeting an intellectual challenge.

Editorial Address:
Springer-Verlag New York
175 Fifth Avenue
New York, NY 10010

National Science Teachers
  Association
1840 Wilson Boulevard
Arlington, VA 22201
703-243-7100
Fax: 703-243-7177

Ordering Address:
Springer-Verlag New York
P.O. Box 2485
Secaucus, NJ 07096
800-SPRINGER
or 201-348-4033

Audience: M/F, ages 11–16
Subject: Spanish language,
sports, TV, film, pop, teen
culture, Spanish and Latin
American culture
Circulation: 90,000
Distribution: Schools
Editor: Marta Giddings
Publisher: Mary Glasgow
Magazines (Scholastic Inc.)
Cost: $6.95 (6 issues)

¿Que Tal?

is written in Spanish for teenagers learning Spanish at school. It covers topics that the age group can relate to while at the same time introducing information and cultural details so that readers learn language and background for the countries where Spanish is spoken. Its goal is to make Spanish come alive for its readers.

Editorial & Ordering Address:
Mary Glasgow Magazines
Commonwealth House
1–19 New Oxford Street
London, England WC1A 1NU
441-71-4219050
Fax: 441-71-4219052

Racing for Kids

is a monthly magazine that seeks to make reading fun for kids interested in racing. Readers can learn about famous race-car drivers and other personalities from NASCAR, Monster Trucks, Sprint Cars, Indy Cars, drag or sports-car racing. Readers are invited to active participation with games, contests, letters, or their own stories or artwork.

Audience: M/F, ages 4–16
Subject: Automobile racing
Circulation: 20,000
Distribution: Homes (75%);
* schools (25%)*
Editor: Gary McCredie
Publisher: John Bickford Sr.
Cost: $3.00/issue; $19.95/yr.
* (12 issues)*
Sample: Call or write
Readers' Work Published:
* Artwork, short stories,*
* poetry*

Editorial & Ordering Address:
Racing for Kids, LLC
P.O. Box 192
Concord, NC 28026-0192
704-786-7132
Fax: 704-795-4460
Orders: 800-443-3020

R-A-D-A-R

is a Sunday school take home paper for children in grades 3–6. *R-A-D-A-R* correlates with the Sunday school curriculum for that age group published by Standard Publishing.

Audience: M/F, ages 8–12
Subject: Making the truth of
* God's word the guide of*
* children's lives*
Circulation: 112,000
Distribution: Sunday schools
* (95%); homes, individuals*
* (5%)*
Editor: Elaina Meyers
Publisher: Mark Taylor
Cost: $12.50/yr. (52 issues)
Sample: Send SASE (business
* size with 1 U.S. 1st class*
* stamp) for 2 samples,*
* guidelines, theme list*
Readers' Work Published:
* Letters, stories*

Editorial & Ordering Address:
Standard Publishing
8121 Hamilton Avenue
Cincinnati, OH 45230
513-931-4050
Fax: 513-931-0904

Radio Control Car Action

offers exciting and stimulating articles and feature stories on the compelling world of radio-controlled cars and trucks. R/C electronics and modeling techniques are covered in every issue.

Audience: M, teens
Subject: Radio control car
* hobbyists*
Circulation: 90,000
Distribution: Newsstands
* (39%); subscriptions*
* (51%); dealers (10%)*
Editor: Frank Masi
Publisher: Air Age Publishing
Cost: $3.95/issue; $29.95/yr.
* (12 issues)*
Sample: Write RC Car
* Action at ordering address*
Readers' Work Published:
* Letters to editor, tips*

Editorial Address:
Air Age Publishing
251 Danbury Road
Wilton, CT 06897
203-431-9000
Fax: 203-762-9803

Ordering Address:
Kable News Fulfillment
P.O. Box 427
Mt. Morris, IL 61054
800-877-5169

Rainbow

is an educational and entertainment magazine for children and young people, produced and published in Kenya since 1976. An African animal, a plant, a musician, and news from Kenya and the world are featured each month. The range of subjects includes African folktales, cartoon strips, jokes, riddles and puzzles, and an awareness of global affairs.

Audience: M/F, ages 10–16
Subject: General interest
Distribution: Subscriptions, retail sales
Editor: Fleur Ng'weno
Publisher: Stellagraphics Limited
Cost: US$30.00/air mail; $15.00/surface mail
Sample: Send $5.00

Editorial & Ordering Address:
Stellagraphics Limited
P.O. Box 42271
Nairobi, Kenya
254-2-724166
Fax: 254-2-222555

Ranger Rick

is dedicated to helping children gain a greater understanding and appreciation of nature. It covers a range of natural history subjects with personalized adventures, animal life histories, fiction, photo/caption stories, how-to articles, jokes and riddles, crafts, plays, and poetry. This 48-page monthly magazine is a benefit of membership in the Ranger Rick Nature Club.

Audience: M/F, ages 6–12
Subject: Nature, environment, outdoors
Circulation: 850,000
Distribution: Homes
Editor: Gerry Bishop
Publisher: National Wildlife Federation
Cost: $15.00 (12 issues)
Sample: Contact editor; $2.15
Readers' Work Published: Letters, questions

Editorial & Ordering Address:
National Wildlife Federation
8925 Leesburg Pike
Vienna, VA 22184-0001
703-790-4000
Fax: 703-442-7332

react

through vigorous journalism, provides quality information to help its readers react (emphasis on ACT) with confidence and compassion in a complex world. *react* is truly an interactive magazine—every page of the magazine encourages readers to respond and interact via e-mail, snail mail, fax, or telephone. It also has an electronic edition, *virtually react*, on the World Wide Web.

Audience: M/F, ages 12–15
Subject: Sports, entertainment, news for and about teens
Circulation: 4.2 million
Distribution: Homes (90%); schools (10%)
Editor: Lee Kravitz
Publisher: Carlo Vittorini, Parade Publications
Cost: Available through newspaper or NIE subscription
Sample: Contact Dennie Hughes at 212-450-0940 (single sample is free)
Readers' Work Published: Letters, essays, jokes, and art

Editorial & Ordering Address:
Parade Publications
711 Third Avenue
15th Floor
New York, NY 10017
212-450-0900
Fax: 212-450-0978
E-mail: editor@react.com

READ Magazine

Audience: M/F, grades 6–12
Subject: Reading, Social Studies, and English
Circulation: 350,000
Distribution: Schools
Editor: Ted Hoey
Publisher: Richard J. LeBrasseur
Cost: $8.65/subscription (18 issues) for 10 or more subscriptions
Sample: Contact customer service

is designed for use in English and reading classes. Every issue contains a play and a short story, word games, logic puzzles, and ideas for student poems. Two pages are devoted to student writing. The accompanying teacher's guide has background and discussion material, plus writing ideas and reproducible masters devoted to various English, literature, and reading skills.

Editorial Address:
Weekly Reader Corp.
P.O. Box 2791
Middletown, CT 06457-9291
860-638-2400
Fax: 860-346-5826

Ordering Address:
Weekly Reader Corp.
3001 Cindel Drive
Delran, NJ 08370
800-446-3355

Sail

Audience: M/F, ages 12–adult
Subject: Sailing
Circulation: 184,000
Distribution: Newsstands
Editor: Patience Wales
Publisher: Donald Macaulay
Cost: $2.50/issue; $19.95/yr. (12 issues)
Sample: On written request ($3.00)

seeks to help the neophyte master the basics of racing and cruising by encouraging a lifelong, pervasive love of the sport. *Sail* makes sailing accessible. It attempts to welcome new sailors and help them find places to sail through clubs, chartering, and community centers. Service is a large part of *Sail's* attraction.

Editorial & Ordering Address:
Cahners Publishing Company
275 Washington Street
Newton, MA 02158-1630
617-720-8600

Scholastic Action Magazine

Audience: M/F, ages 13–18
Subject: High-interest, inspirational stories about issues relevant to teenagers struggling in school
Circulation: 170,000
Distribution: Schools
Editor: Patrick Daly
Publisher: Scholastic Inc.
Cost: $6.95/student/yr. (14 issues)
Sample: Request sample from ordering address
Readers' Work Published: Letters, point of view opinion pieces

is a high-interest, low vocabulary magazine. Its plays and articles seek to motivate students to read as well as provide information that will help its readers—many of whom are at risk of dropping out of school—succeed at school, at home, and in life.

Editorial Address:
Scholastic Inc.
555 Broadway
New York, NY 10012
212-343-6100

Ordering Address:
Scholastic Inc.
2931 E. McCarty Street
P.O. Box 3710
Jefferson City, MO 65102-3710
800-631-1586

Scholastic Art

Audience: M/F, jr. high, middle, high school students
Subject: Art
Circulation: 200,000
Distribution: Schools
Editor: Margaret Howlett
Publisher: Scholastic Inc.
Cost: $6.95/student for 10 or more subscriptions (6 issues)
Sample: Call 800-631-1586 for free sample copy
Readers' Work Published: Students' artwork

introduces teenagers to fine arts in an interesting, clear, understandable, relevant way. It seeks to link art history to the student's own classroom work. While the magazine is designed as supplementary material, each issue and its accompanying teaching guide may serve as a unit on a particular art element or principle.

Editorial Address:
Scholastic Inc.
555 Broadway
New York, NY 10012
212-343-6100

Ordering Address:
Scholastic Inc.
2931 E. McCarty Street
P.O. Box 3710
Jefferson City, MO 65102-3710
800-631-1586

Scholastic Choices

Audience: M/F, grades 7–12
Subject: Personal development and living skills
Circulation: 240,000
Distribution: Schools
Editor: Lauren Tarshis
Publisher: Scholastic Inc.
Cost: $5.95/student for 10 or more subscriptions
Sample: Available to teachers and librarians

is designed to be of great interest to teens while helping teachers navigate through some of the more complex issues relating to teen life: relationships, emotions, family life, health, and sexuality. Each issue includes a mix of articles, plus one package devoted to a theme, such as family life, prejudice, fitting in, or gender stereotypes.

Editorial Address:
Scholastic Inc.
555 Broadway
New York, NY 10012
212-343-6100

Ordering Address:
Scholastic Inc.
2931 E. McCarty Street
P.O. Box 3710
Jefferson City, MO 65102-3710
800-631-1586

Scholastic Dynamath

Audience: M/F, grades 5–6
Subject: Math
Circulation: 300,000
Distribution: Schools
Editor: Joe D'Agnese
Publisher: Scholastic Inc.
Cost: $6.50/student for 10 or more subscriptions (8 issues)
Sample: Available to teachers and librarians

is a 16-page classroom magazine used as a supplement for math programs. It seeks to engage readers in mathematics by presenting in a humorous format activities such as word problems, computation, and test preparation.

Editorial Address:
Scholastic Inc.
555 Broadway
New York, NY 10012
212-343-6100
E-mail: dynamath@ scholastic.com

Ordering Address:
Scholastic Inc.
2931 E. McCarty Street
P.O. Box 3710
Jefferson City, MO 65102-3710
800-631-1586

Scholastic Math

Audience: M/F, grades 7–9
Subject: Math
Circulation: 230,000
Distribution: Schools
Editor: Sarah Jane Brian
Publisher: Scholastic Inc.
Cost: $7.50/student for 10 or more subscriptions (14 issues)
Sample: Available to teachers and librarians
Readers' Work Published: Puzzles, brain teasers, published math mistakes

is a classroom magazine designed as a supplement to the math curriculum. Each issue includes articles that provide a format for problem solving, computation, statistics, consumer math, real-life applications, career math, test-taking preparation, and critical reasoning skills.

Editorial Address:
Scholastic Inc.
555 Broadway
New York, NY 10012
212-343-6435
Fax: 212-343-6333
E-mail: mathmag@scholastic.com

Ordering Address:
Scholastic Inc.
2931 E. McCarty Street
P.O. Box 3710
Jefferson City, MO 65102-3710
800-631-1586

Scholastic News

Audience: M/F, grades 1–6
Subject: News, current events
Distribution: Schools
Editor: Tamara Rubin
Publisher: Scholastic Inc.
Cost: $2.75/student (grades 1–2); $2.90/student (grades 3–6)
Readers' Work Published: Mostly letters to the editor

is a weekly classroom newspaper, published in six separate editions for children in grades 1–6. Each edition is planned and written at the age-appropriate level to help students understand major world and national news. The teacher's edition provides background information, discussion questions, activities, skills reproducibles, and color teaching posters.

Editorial Address:
Scholastic Inc.
555 Broadway
New York, NY 10012
212-343-6100
Fax: 212-343-6484

Ordering Address:
Scholastic Inc.
2931 E. McCarty Street
P.O. Box 3710
Jefferson City, MO 65102-3710
800-631-1586

Scholastic Scope

Audience: M/F, junior high and high school students
Subject: Language arts
Circulation: 470,000
Distribution: Schools
Editor: Hugh Roon
Publisher: Richard Robinson
Cost: $6.95/student for 10 or more subscriptions (20 issues); $1.25/issue
Sample: Send SASE and $1.25 to editorial address

is a classroom-based language arts magazine that presents a combination of classics and contemporary works in an effort to supplement curricular materials. Issues typically include a play that can be done in class, a short story, suggested reading lists, innovative writing exercises, and other skills builders.

Editorial Address:
Scholastic Inc.
555 Broadway
New York, NY 10012
212-343-6100

Ordering Address:
Scholastic Inc.
2931 E. McCarty Street
P.O. Box 3710
Jefferson City, MO 65102-3710
800-631-1586

Scholastic Sprint

Audience: M/F, grades 4–6 with grade 2 or 3 reading level
Subject: Language arts
Distribution: Schools
Editor: Karen Glenn
Publisher: Scholastic Inc.
Cost: $5.95/student for 10 or more subscriptions

is a classroom magazine for students in grades 4–6 with a reading level of grades 2–3. It is designed as a supplement for language arts classes for students with special learning needs. It features an integrated approach to the development of basic language skills including reading, writing, vocabulary, and thinking.

Editorial Address:
Scholastic Inc.
555 Broadway
New York, NY 10012
212-343-6100

Ordering Address:
Scholastic Inc.
2931 E. McCarty Street
P.O. Box 3710
Jefferson City, MO 65102-3710
800-631-1586

Scholastic Update

Audience: M/F, grades 8–12
Subject: Social studies, current events
Circulation: 85,000
Distribution: Schools, classrooms
Editor: Steve C. Manning
Publisher: Scholastic Inc.
Cost: $7.50/yr. (14 issues); $4.50/semester for 10+; $11.45/student 1–9; $24.00/teachers
Sample: Available to teachers, librarians, individuals
Readers' Work Published: Letters, opinion

a current-affairs social studies magazine presenting in-depth facts and opinions aimed at helping teenage readers shape their views on the most important global and domestic issues of our day. Each issue offers a mix of survey pieces, teen profiles, interactive features, maps, charts, and graphs—plus a teaching guide.

Editorial Address:
Scholastic Inc.
555 Broadway
New York, NY 10012
212-343-6271
Fax: 212-343-6333
E-mail: updatemag@scholastic.com

Ordering Address:
Scholastic Inc.
2931 E. McCarty Street
P.O. Box 3710
Jefferson City, MO 65102-3710
800-631-1586

School Magazine

Audience: M/F, ages 8–12
Subject: Literary—stories, poems, plays
Circulation: 200,000
Distribution: Schools (97%); other (3%)
Editor: Jonathan Shaw
Publisher: New South Wales Department of School Education
Cost: AUS$7.00/yr. plus $25.00 postage (outside Australia) (10 issues)
Sample: On written request
Readers' Work Published: Letters

is actually four magazines, *Countdown* for 8- to 9-year olds, *Blast Off* for 9- to 10-year olds, *Orbit* for 10- to 11-year olds, and *Touchdown* for advanced elementary school grades.

Editorial & Ordering Address:
Private Bag 3
Ryde, NSW
Australia 2112
02-9808-9598
Fax: 02-9808-9588

School Mates

Audience: M/F, ages 5+
Subject: Chess
Circulation: 28,000
Distribution: Homes (90%);
* schools (10%)*
Editor: Jay Hastings
Publisher: United States Chess
* Federation*
Cost: $2.50/issue; $10.00/yr.
* w/USCF membership to*
* ages 19 and under;*
* $10.50/yr. to others*
* (6 issues)*
Sample: Upon request
Readers' Work Published:
* Letters, art, photos, puz-*
* zles, stories, poems, chess*
* games they have won*

seeks to help young people learn and enjoy the game of chess. It features stories about famous players and outstanding young players, as well as their winning games and tips on how to play better chess. Each issue offers a lesson on a specific theme, along with quizzes, puzzles, reader letters, tournament listings, and news items.

Editorial & Ordering Address:
U.S. Chess Federation
186 Route 9W
New Windsor, NY 12553
914-562-8350
Fax: 914-561-2437
800-388-KING
E-mail: USCF@delphi.com

Schuss

Audience: M/F, ages 11–16
Subject: German language,
* sports, TV, film, pop, teen*
* culture, Germanic culture*
Circulation: 50,000
Distribution: Schools
Editor: Miroslav Imbresevic
Publisher: Mary Glasgow
* Magazines*
Cost: $6.95/subscription;
* (6 issues)*
Sample: Free sample from
* ordering address*
Readers' Work Published:
* Cartoons, quizzes, compe-*
* titions, topical articles,*
* written by native speakers.*

is written in German for teenagers learning German at school. It covers topics that the age group can relate to while at the same time introducing information and cultural details so that readers learn language and background for the countries where German is spoken. Its goal is to make German come alive for its readers.

Editorial Address:
Mary Glasgow Magazines
Commonwealth House
1–19 New Oxford Street
London, England WC1A 1NU
441-71-4219050
Fax: 441-71-4219052

Ordering Address:
Scholastic Inc.
2931 E. McCarty Street
P.O. Box 3710
Jefferson City, MO 65102-3710
800-631-1586

Science News: The Weekly Newsmagazine of Science

Audience: M/F, high school
* and up*
Subject: Physical science, bio-
* logical science, behavior*
Circulation: 250,000
Distribution: Subscriptions
Editor: Julie Ann Miller
Publisher: Donald Harless
Cost: $49.50/yr. (52 issues)
Sample: Send request with
* address*

focuses on new discoveries in science, the personalities behind the discoveries, and the implications of the discoveries for the scientific and industrial sectors.

Editorial Address:
1719 N Street NW
Washington, DC 20036
202-785-2255
Fax: 202-659-0365
E-mail: scinews@scisvc.org

Ordering Address:
P.O. Box 1925
Marion, OH 43305
800-347-6969

Science Weekly

Audience: M/F, grades K–8
Subject: Science and technology
Circulation: 200,000
Distribution: Schools (95%); other (5%)
Editor: Deborah Lazar
Publisher: Claude Mayberry
Cost: $4.95/yr. (20 or more subscriptions); $9.95/yr. (under 20)
Sample: Upon request

is designed to motivate students and to help them develop an awareness of science and technology in the world around them. Each issue is based on a single science topic and is available on seven different reading levels. Every issue integrates hands-on-labs, language arts, mathematics, and critical thinking skills activities in a way that makes scientific exploration both fun and rewarding for your students.

Editorial Address:
Science Weekly, Inc.
2141 Industrial Parkway
Suite 202
Silver Spring, MD 20904
301-680-8804
Fax: 301-680-9240

Ordering Address:
Science Weekly
P.O. Box 70638
Chevy Chase, MD 20813
800-4-WEEKLY

Science World

Audience: M/F, grades 7–10
Subject: Science
Circulation: 350,000
Distribution: Schools
Editor: Karen McNulty
Publisher: Scholastic Inc.
Cost: $7.50 each for orders of 10 or more (14 issues)
Sample: Available with SASE

seeks to supplement the lessons of the science curriculum. Published biweekly during the school year, this 24-page publication includes brief news items and several features on current research in the life, earth (including astronomy and space), physical, and health sciences. "Do-it-yourself" science activities lead readers to investigate key concepts in the articles.

Editorial Address:
Scholastic Inc.
555 Broadway
New York, NY 10012-3999
212-343-6100
E-mail: scienceworld@ scholastic.com

Ordering Address:
Scholastic Inc.
2931 E. McCarty Street
P.O. Box 3710
Jefferson City, MO 65102-9957
314-636-8890

Scienceland

Audience: M/F, ages 5–10
Subject: Nature, physical science
Circulation: 15,000
Distribution: Schools, home schoolers (90%); parent-teachers (10%)
Editor: Albert H. Matano
Publisher: Albert H. Matano
Cost: $36.00/yr. (4 issues)

is designed to integrate the benefits of a picture book, reading book, and workbook in magazine format, using photos and illustrations to nurture scientific thinking through content reading. It serves the kindergartener being read to, the 1st grader learning the alphabet, the 2nd and 3rd grader learning to read and to the 5th and 6th grader beginning to understand science concepts.

Editorial & Ordering Address:
Scienceland
501 Fifth Avenue
Suite 2108
New York, NY 10017-6107
212-490-2180
Fax: 212-490-2187

Scott Stamp Monthly

Audience: M/F, ages 10–18
Subject: Stamp collecting
Distribution: Subscriptions (90%); newsstands (10%)
Editor: Richard L. Sine

exists to entertain its readers through well-illustrated, interesting, and informative features and how-to articles. The magazine in one form or another has existed for well over 100 years.

Editorial & Ordering Address:
Scott Publishing Company
P.O. Box 828
Sidney, OH 45365

Seedling Series: Short Story International

Audience: M/F, ages 10–13
Subject: Contemporary, unabridged short stories from all lands written by living, indigenous, gifted writers who know their peoples and cultures well
Circulation: 24,000
Distribution: Homes (50%); schools, libraries (50%)
Editor: Sylvia Tankel
Publisher: Sam Tankel
Cost: $4.95/issue; $16.00/yr. (4 issues)
Sample: Free sample to schools and libraries upon written request; $6.20 to others

is a 64-page quarterly which publishes short stories from all over the world that promote and strengthen the reading habit. The stories are selected to appeal to both reluctant readers and avid readers. Similarities and differences of their peers around the globe are emphasized to readers.

Editorial Address:
Short Story International
6 Sheffield Road
Great Neck, NY 11021
516-466-4166

Ordering Address:
Short Story International
P.O. Box 405
Great Neck, NY 11022
516-466-4166

Sesame Street Magazine

Audience: M/F, ages 2–6 and parents
Subject: General interest/stories, games and activities for preschoolers, articles and tips for parents
Distribution: Homes, newsstands
Editor: Rebecca Herman
Publisher: Nina Link
Cost: $13.97/yr.

features stories, games, and activities that introduce the alphabet, numbers, and simple problem-solving skills, and reinforce positive social skills using characters and settings from the television program. The accompanying parents' guide includes tips, articles on child development and parenting skills and strategies, and suggestions in reference to *Sesame Street Magazine*.

Editorial Address:
Children's Television
   Workshop
One Lincoln Plaza
New York, NY 10023
212-595-3456

Ordering Address:
P.O. Box 52000
Boulder, CO 80321-2000

Audience: M/F, ages 9–13
*Subject: Religion/Jewish-
   American*
Circulation: 15,000
Distribution: Homes, schools
Editor: Gerald H. Grayson
Publisher: Gerald H. Grayson
*Cost: $14.95/yr.; $9.00/yr. 10
   or more subscriptions*
Sample: Send $1.00

Shofar

is an interactive magazine for American Jewish children. It contains profiles of Jewish celebrities and sports figures, Jewish current events, contests, fiction, puzzles, plays, poems, and artwork. Ready-to-use lessons and family education programs are provided free.

Editorial & Ordering Address:
43 Northcote Drive
Melville, NY 11747
516-643-4598
Fax: 516-643-4598 (call first)
E-mail: graysonpsc@aol.com

Audience: M/F, ages 3–7
*Subject: Poetry, literature,
   storytelling, songs*
Circulation: 500
*Distribution: Homes (90%);
   schools, libraries (10%)*
*Editor: Jack Nestor & Arlene
   Furman*
*Publisher: Shoofly, Inc., Jack
   Nestor*
*Cost: $9.95/cassette;
   $29.95/yr. (4 cassettes)*
*Sample: Call or write for free
   sample*
*Readers' Work Published:
   Child's drawing featured
   on cover*

Shoofly: An Audiomagazine for Children

is dedicated to the celebration of contemporary children's poetry and literature and strives to introduce curious young minds to the wonder and magic of poetry and language. More than just a story tape, each surprising issue is filled with all new material from an eclectic mix of authors and performers from around the country. Discover tomorrow's children's classics today in *Shoofly*!

Editorial & Ordering Address:
Shoofly
P.O. Box 1237
Carrboro, NC 27510
919-968-7846
Fax: 919-968-7846
Orders: 800-919-9989

*Audience: M/F, grades K–12
   Montana students*
*Subject: Stories, poems, essays,
   black and white drawings*
Circulation: 2,000
*Distribution: Homes, schools,
   libraries, classrooms*
Editor: Shirley M. Olson
*Publishers: AGATE,
   MATELA, MAEA and
   MT Arts Council, teacher
   organizations*
Cost: $5.00 for annual issue
*Readers' Work Published:
   Stories, poems, essays, black
   and white drawings*

Signatures from Big Sky

seeks to offer an outlet for talented Montana students' art and literary work, to provide student models for classroom teachers' use, and to promote the arts in Montana schools.

Editorial & Ordering Address:
928 Fourth Avenue
Laurel, MT 59044
406-628-7063

Audience: M/F, ages 12–15
South African youth
Subject: Environmental
education
Circulation: 98,000
Editor: Annelé Steinman
Publisher: Department of
Environmental Affairs
Cost: Free for children (send
child's name, address, and
age) (4 issues)
Sample: Send name & address
Readers' Work Published:
Stories and projects

Skipper

published in Afrikaans and English, provides environmental educational information to make youth aware of the environment and to give them practical information to improve their living environment. The magazine includes comics, drawings, and competitions. This 24-page, quarterly magazine first appeared 13 years ago.

Editorial & Ordering Address:
Department of Environment Affairs
Private Bag X447
Pretoria, 0001, South Africa
012-310-3445
Fax: 012-322-2476
E-mail: med-as@ozone.pwv.gov.za

Audience: M/F, 7–16 years
Subject: Cultural diversity,
international understand-
ing, social issues
Circulation: 2,500
Distribution: Homes, schools,
libraries, newsstands
Editor: Arun Narayan Toké
Publisher: Skipping Stones, Inc.
Cost: $5.00/issue; $20.00/yr.
(5 issues); $30.00/yr.
institutions (5 issues)
Sample: $5.00; or $4.00 with
SASE and 98¢ postage
Readers' Work Published:
Letters, penpals, stories,
poems, riddles, essays, pho-
tos, art, Annual Youth
Honor Awards

Skipping Stones: A Multicultural Children's Magazine

is a multilingual, environmentally aware magazine designed to let children from diverse backgrounds share their experiences, cultures, languages, and creative expressions. Features have included photos by Soviet youth, songs from Japan, India, and Africa, and environmental games from Native Americans and Mexicans. *Skipping Stones* is printed on recycled paper and is distributed worldwide.

Editorial & Ordering Address:
P.O. Box 3939
Eugene, OR 97403-0939
541-342-4956

Audience: M/F, all ages
Subject: Astronomy and space
science
Circulation: 95,000
Editor: Leif J. Robinson
Publisher: Sky Publishing
Corporation
Cost: $2.95/issue; $27.00/yr.
(12 issues)
Sample: $2.95

Sky & Telescope

seeks to be the world's leading source of accurate and timely news and information on astronomy and space science. Each issue contains sky maps, photographs, and instructions for sky-gazers. With reports on the latest discoveries from the world's great observatories and space telescopes, *Sky & Telescope* delivers the best ideas and images from astronomers and astrophotographers.

Editorial & Ordering Address:
Sky Publishing Corporation
P.O. Box 9111
Belmont, MA 02178-9111
617-864-7360
Fax: 617-864-6117

Slap

Audience: M/F, ages 13–20 active youth
Subject: Skateboarding, music, fashion, attitude
Circulation: 50,000+
Distribution: Newsstands (80%); homes (20%)
Editor: Kevin J. Thatcher, Associate Publisher
Publisher: High Speed Productions, Inc.
Cost: $1.95/issue; $16.50/yr.
Sample: Inquire for free sample and sticker
Readers' Work Published: Letters, stories, drawings

is the latest, hippest magazine for the new school crew into skateboarding, street fashion, and the latest sounds. *Slap* combines a crisp attitude with photos of top skateboarders, interviews, product and fashion updates, and hip-hop and rock reviews.

Editorial & Ordering Address:
High Speed Productions, Inc.
1303 Underwood
P.O. Box 884570
San Francisco, CA 94124
415-822-3083
Fax: 415-822-8359

Soccer JR. Magazine

Audience: M/F, ages 8–16
Subject: Soccer skills, tactics, fiction, health, humor
Circulation: 100,000
Distribution: Homes (85%); promotional (10%); newsstands (5%)
Editor: Joe Provey
Publisher: Tom Mindrum
Cost: $16.97/yr.
Sample: Send $3.95 for postage and handling
Readers' Work Published: Stories, artwork

readers are girls and boys who love to play soccer. *Soccer JR.* is designed to be a place where kids can learn about their sport, become better players, and discover who the world's best players are. Each issue uses games, cartoons, and quizzes to help kids learn other life skills like injury prevention, fitness training, nutrition, teamwork, and leadership.

Editorial Address:
Triplepoint, Inc.
27 Unquowa Road
Fairfield, CT 06430
203-259-5766
Fax: 203-254-2966

Ordering Address:
Soccer JR. Magazine
P.O. Box 420442
Palm Coast, FL 32142

Spaceflight

Audience: M/F, all ages
Subject: Space and astronautics
Circulation: 8,000
Distribution: Newsstands, memberships, library subscriptions
Editor: G.V. Groves
Publisher: British Interplanetary Society
Cost: $6.00/issue; $69.00/yr. (12 issues)
Sample: Available on request

seeks to combine the standards of a technical magazine with a presentation that is attractive to a wide international readership. It is widely referenced and is a prime source of information in the space and space-related fields. Its contents include: international space report, missions reports, interviews, book notices, correspondence, and feature articles.

Editorial & Ordering Address:
British Interplanetary Society
27/29 South Lambeth Road
London, England SW8 1SZ
071-735-3160
Fax: 071-820-1504
E-mail: bis@cix.compulink.co.uk

Spider: The Magazine for Children

Audience: M/F, ages 6–9
Subject: Stories, poems, activities
Circulation: 90,000
Editor: Marianne Carus, Editor-in-Chief
Publisher: Robert W. Harper
Cost: $4.00/issue; $32.97/yr. (12 months)
Sample: Send $4.00 to Mary Beth Miklavcik at editorial address

introduces 6- to 9-year-old children to the highest quality stories, poems, illustrations, articles, and activities. It was created to foster in beginning readers a love of reading and discovery that will last a lifetime. A cast of bug characters traipse through the margins, providing humorous commentary and explaining difficult concepts.

Editorial Address:
Spider
315 Fifth Street
Peru, IL 61354
815-224-6656

Ordering Address:
Spider
P.O. Box 7435
Red Oak, IA 51591-4435
800-827-0227

Sports Illustrated for Kids

Audience: M/F, ages 8+
Subject: Sports
Circulation: 934,248
Distribution: Homes (70%); schools (27%); newsstands (3%)
Editor: Neil Cohen
Cost: $2.95/issue; $27.95/yr. (12 issues)
Sample: Send check for $2.95 to Birmingham address; librarians and teachers, call 800-633-8628
Readers' Work Published: Letters, artwork

presents sports-oriented subjects in a 4-color magazine format. It introduces young readers to professional and amateur sports figures. This publication includes features on athletes who began their careers at the same age range as the readers. Regular departments include sports cards, legends, puzzles, activities, and Tips from the Pros.

Editorial Address:
Time Inc. Magazine Co.
1271 Sixth Avenue
New York, NY 10020
212-522-KIDS
Fax: 212-522-0120

Ordering Address:
Time Inc. Magazine Co.
P.O. Box 830609
Birmingham, AL 35283-0609
800-334-2229 U.S. and Canada

Stone Soup: The Magazine by Young Writers and Artists

Audience: M/F, ages 6–13
Subject: Writing and art by children
Circulation: 20,000
Distribution: Schools (40%); homes (35%); newsstands (20%); public libraries (5%)
Editor: Gerry Mandel
Publisher: Children's Art Foundation
Cost: $26.00/yr. (5 issues)
Sample: Write or call; free for single sample
Readers' Work Published: Stories, poems, art

believes that by publishing rich, heartfelt work by young people the world over, it can stir the imaginations of its readers and inspire young writers and artists to create.

Editorial & Ordering Address:
Children's Art Foundation
P.O. Box 83
Santa Cruz, CA 95063
408-426-5557 or 800-447-4569
Fax: 408-426-1161
E-mail: editor@stonesoup.com

Audience: M/F, ages 4–8
Subject: Biblically-sound reading and activities
Circulation: 5,000
Distribution: Churches (96%); homes (4%)
Editor: Miriam R. Shank
Publisher: Christian Light Publications, Inc.
Cost: $9.00/yr.
Sample: Send a 6" × 9" SASE with 52¢ postage

Story Mates

a Sunday school take-home paper, is intended to help readers to revere God as Father and Creator, accept His authoritative Word, and appreciate His great plan of salvation. *Story Mates'* stories and activities exemplify conservative Mennonite interpretation and applications of Biblical teachings.

Editorial & Ordering Address:
Christian Light Publications
P.O. Box 1126
Harrisonburg, VA 22801
703-434-0768

Audience: M/F, grades 3–5 and teachers
Subject: Literature
Circulation: 200,000
Distribution: Classrooms, homes, libraries
Editor: Tamara Hanneman
Publisher: Scholastic Inc.
Cost: $3.95/student per school yr.; teacher's edition is free with order of 10 or more subscriptions (6 issues/school yr.)
Readers' Work Published: Children's book reviews, letters

Storyworks Magazine

seeks to turn kids on to the wonderful and exciting world of literature. Each issue features work by top children's authors. In addition to short stories, nonfiction, plays, and poetry, the magazine publishes student-written book reviews, word games, writing activities, author interviews, and news briefs about books. The teacher's edition provides literature-based teaching ideas to use in the classroom.

Editorial Address:
Scholastic Inc.
555 Broadway
New York, NY 10012
212-343-6298
Fax: 212-343-6333

Ordering Address:
Scholastic Inc.
2931 E. McCarty Street
P.O. Box 3710
Jefferson City, MO 65101-3710
800-631-1586

Audience: M/F, ages 13–19
Subject: Contemporary issues facing Christian teenagers
Circulation: 35,000
Distribution: Churches, Sunday schools
Editor: Heather E. Wallace
Publisher: Mark Taylor
Cost: $11.49/yr. (52 issues)
Sample: Send SASE to editor
Readers' Work Published: Poetry, personal experiences, stories

Straight Magazine

is a weekly magazine for Christian teenagers, distributed through churches. It's designed to correlate with Standard Publishing's Young Teen and Youth Bible School lessons.

Editorial & Ordering Address:
Standard Publishing
8121 Hamilton Avenue
Cincinnati, OH 45231
513-931-4050
Fax: 513-931-0904
Orders: 800-543-1301

Student Series: Short Story International

seeks to fill the need for enticing stories for teenagers to broaden their horizons and to provide insights into the peoples of the world with whom they must live. In addition, stories are selected from all the world with the aim of promoting and strengthening the reading habit.

Audience: M/F, ages 13–18
Subject: Short stories, language arts
Circulation: 23,000
Distribution: Homes (50%); schools, libraries (50%)
Editor: Sylvia Tankel
Publisher: Sam Tankel
Cost: $5.75/issue; $21.00/yr. (4 issues)
Sample: Free sample to schools/libraries upon written request; $6.50 to others

Editorial Address:
Short Story International
6 Sheffield Road
Great Neck, NY 11021
516-466-4166

Ordering Address:
Short Story International
P.O. Box 405
Great Neck, NY 11022
516-466-4166

Superman and Batman Magazine

focuses on the Superman and Batman characters. The magazine seeks to interact with kids by including excerpts from *The Daily Planet* newspaper; the Hero File, a complete profile of D.C. Comics' leading characters; Backstage at D.C. Comics, interviews with the people behind the comic books, character puzzles, and pull-outs.

Audience: M/F, ages 6–12
Subject: Entertainment
Circulation: 250,000
Distribution: Newsstands, subscriptions
Editor: Adam Philips
Publisher: Donald E. Welsh, Welsh Publishing Group
Cost: $1.95/issue (4 issues/yr.)
Readers' Work Published: Letters, artwork

Editorial Address:
Marvel Entertainment
    Group, Inc.
87 Park Avenue
New York, NY 10016
212-687-0680
Fax: 212-986-3746

Ordering Address:
P.O. Box 7545
Red Oak, IA 51591
515-243-4543

SuperScience Blue Edition

is a classroom magazine for students in grades 4–6, created as a science supplement for elementary classes. This 16-page, hands-on magazine includes a bimonthly poster (one per class) and is issued monthly during the school year to introduce students to science through classroom activities.

Audience: M/F, grades 4–6
Subject: Science
Distribution: Schools
Editor: Nancy Finton
Publisher: Scholastic Inc.
Cost: $5.95/10 or more subscriptions (8 issues)
Sample: Teachers and librarians, contact 800-631-1586

Editorial Address:
Scholastic Inc.
555 Broadway
New York, NY 10012-3999
212-343-6469
Fax: 212-343-6333
E-mail: superscibl@aol.com

Ordering Address:
Scholastic Inc.
2931 E. McCarty Street
P.O. Box 3710
Jefferson City, MO 65101-3710
800-631-1586

Audience: M/F, grades 1–3
Subject: Science
Circulation: 200,000
Distribution: Schools
Editor: Kathy Burkett
Publisher: Scholastic Inc.
Cost: $4.95/10 or more sub-
*   scriptions (6 issues)*
Sample: Call 800-631-1586

SuperScience Red

is a classroom magazine for grades 1–3 and offers primary students an introduction to basic science concepts through fun, hands-on activities. Each 16-page issue is based on a theme and geared to developing critical thinking and logical reasoning skills. The magazine is published 6 times during the school year.

Editorial Address:
Scholastic Inc.
555 Broadway
New York, NY 10012
212-343-6472
Fax: 212-343-6333
E-mail: supersciencered@scholastic.com

Ordering Address:
Scholastic Inc.
2931 E. McCarty Street
P.O. Box 3710
Jefferson City, MO 65101-3710
800-631-1586

Audience: M, ages 10–50
Subject: Surfing
Circulation: 105,000
Distribution: Homes (50%);
*   newsstands (50%)*
Editor: Steve Hawk
Publisher: Court Overin
Cost: $3.95/issue; $20.95/yr.
*   (12 issues)*
Sample: Write Lisa Boelter at
*   editorial address*

Surfer

is about surfers, for surfers, by surfers. It features stories about beaches and the surfers who use them, profiles on celebrity surfers, announcements of competitions, and first-person accounts of surfing experiences.

Editorial Address:
Box 1028
Dana Point, CA 92629
714-496-5922
Fax: 714-496-7849

Ordering Address:
Neo Data
P.O. Box 58122
Boulder, CO 80322-8122

Audience: M/F, ages 5–12
Subject: General interest
Circulation: 95,000
Distribution: Homes (80%);
*   schools, libraries (20%)*
Editor: Jeanne Palmer
Publisher: Roger Heegaard
Cost: $14.95/yr. (6 issues)
Readers' Work Published:
*   Letters, artwork, activities*

Surprises: Activities for Today's Kids and Parents

aims to be an educational activity magazine that inspires elementary-age children to learn while having fun. The mission of *Surprises* is to educate, entertain, and enlighten children through active learning—learning by doing.

Editorial Address:
Children's Surprises, Inc.
275 Market Street
Suite 521
Minneapolis, MN 55405
612-937-8345

Ordering Address:
Children's Surprises, Inc.
P.O. Box 20471
Bloomington, MN 55405

Taghna T-tfal

has been published regularly since 1980 as a follow-up of the International year held in 1979 and offers Maltese children a magazine of their own. Its aim is to provide them with literature, general knowledge, religion, and love of nature and the environment.

Audience: M/F, ages 6–12
Subject: General knowledge, religion, nature, games, stories
Circulation: 15,000
Distribution: Schools of Malta & Gozo
Editor: Mary Puli
Publisher: Gutenberg Press
Cost: $.10/issue (9 issues)
Sample: free
Readers' Work Published: Stories, rhymes, jokes

Editorial & Ordering Address:
Malta Catholic Action
Catholic Institute
Floriana, Malta VLT 16

Talents

is for all those involved in third-level education, aimed at students or future students of universities, IUT, BTS, preparatory schools, or polytechnics. *Talents* is both an accurate, involving guide to student life and all its difficulties, and also a real news magazine, with big features on international affairs, cinema, culture, and leisure activities.

Audience: Young adults and students
Subject: Guide to student life, real news magazine (cinema, culture, leisure)
Circulation: 56,000
Distribution: Subscriptions, schools, newsstands
Editor: Didier Williame
Publisher: Bayard Presse
Cost: 15 FF/issue; 289 FF/yr.

Editorial Address:
Bayard Presse
3 rue Bayard
Paris 75008, France
331-44-356060
Fax: 331-44-35604

Ordering Address:
Bayard Presse International
BP 12
99505 Paris Entreprise France
331-44-216000

Tapori

encourages children from all social and cultural backgrounds to share their experiences and ideas on how to fight extreme poverty. Having a home, family, education, and health care is something that is taken for granted sometimes. Yet, if it is so essential for each of us, how could we believe it is not for others? "We want all children to have the same chances" is the *Tapori* motto.

Audience: M/F, ages 6–13
Subject: Human dignity; understanding and respect in order to build a better world
Circulation: 2,000
Distribution: Homes (50%); schools, libraries (50%)
Editor: Francaise Sleeth
Publisher: Tapori/ Fourth World Movement
Cost: $10.00/yr. (10 issues)
Sample: Contact editor by phone, mail, or fax for free sample

Editorial & Ordering Address:
Tapori/ Fourth World Movement
7600 Willow Hill Drive
Landover, MD 20785-4658
301-336-9489

Audience: F, ages 8–18, primarily 12 and 13
Subject: Celebrity teens in the entertainment field
Circulation: 150,000
Distribution: Newsstands, subscriptions
Editor: Karen L. Williams
Cost: $2.99/issue; $19.95/yr. (12 issues)
Readers' Work Published: Photos, letters, celebrity photos taken by fans

Teen Beat

is a magazine for today's teenage girl featuring popular personalities from TV, movies, and music. Regular issue features include interviews, on-set visits, movie previews, celebrity news, contests, and color pin-ups.

Editorial & Ordering Address:
Sterling/McFadden Partnership
233 Park Avenue South
6th Floor
New York, NY 10003
212-979-4880
Fax: 212-979-7342

Audience: M/F, ages 12–19
Subject: Religious inspiration and instruction
Circulation: 60,000
Distribution: Sunday schools (95%); subscriptions (2%)
Editor: Tammy Bicket
Publisher: Gospel Publishing House
Cost: $1.90/quarter (4 issues)
Sample: Send request and SASE
Readers' Work Published: Fiction and/or articles that meet usual editorial needs

Teen Life

is designed to illustrate teens living according to biblical, Assemblies of God-based principles. Its goal is to present interesting fiction and articles that deal with the conflicts, problems, joys, and opportunities teens face.

Editorial & Ordering Address:
Gospel Publishing House
1445 Boonville Avenue
Springfield, MO 65802-1894
417-862-2781, ext. 4359
Fax: 417-862-6059
E-mail: youthcurr@ag.org
Orders: 800-641-4310
Fax: 800-328-0294

Audience: F, high school students
Subject: Fashion, beauty, growing-up issues
Circulation: 1.1 million
Distribution: Homes (66%); newsstands (34%)
Editor: Roxanne Camron
Publishers: Robert MacLeod and Jay Cole
Cost: $2.25/issue; $12.95/yr. (12 issues)
Sample: Send $2.50
Readers' Work Published: Poetry

'Teen Magazine

is designed to serve the total needs of girls 11–17. Editorial content is directed toward service and a wholesome contribution to young America and its future. Focus is on self-improvement in areas of grooming and physical and intellectual development. The publication seeks to provide parents with a common ground of communication with their daughters.

Editorial & Ordering Address:
8490 Sunset Boulevard
Los Angeles, CA 90069
310-854-2950

Teen Power

Audience: M/F, ages 11–15
Subject: Christian living
Distribution: Churches, subscriptions
Editor: Amy Cox
Publisher: Scripture Press Publications
Cost: $8.75/yr.
Sample: Send SASE to editor
Readers' Work Published: True stories, poetry

shows readers how biblical principles for Christian living can be applied to everyday life. We are looking for fresh, creative, true stories, and true-to-life fiction. All must show how God and the Bible are relevant in the lives of today's teens. All must have a clear, spiritual emphasis. Stories that merely have a good moral are not used. They must be realistic, not preachy or talk down to kids. Dialogue should be natural. Resolutions should not be too easy or tacked on.

Editorial & Ordering Address:
Scripture Press Publications, Inc.
4050 Lee Vance View
Colorado Springs, CO 80918
800-708-5550
Orders: 800-323-7543

Teen Times

Audience: M/F, secondary school students
Subject: Family, school, community, and world issues as part of the vocational home economics program
Circulation: 270,000
Distribution: Schools
Editor: Patti Frattarola
Publisher: Future Homemakers of America, Inc.
Cost: Free/members/yr.; $7.00/nonmembers (4 issues)
Readers' Work Published: Comments, poems, artwork, essays

seeks to encourage positive changes and stress leadership qualities. Each issue explores topics like family, volunteering, and careers and is filled with helpful hints, as well as thought-provoking and action ideas. The publication is distributed four times a year as part of Future Homemakers of America membership dues.

Editorial & Ordering Address:
Future Homemakers of America, Inc.
1910 Association Drive
Reston, VA 20191
703-476-4900
Fax: 703-860-2713
E-mail: fhahero.access.digex.net

Audience: F, ages 12–19
Subject: "Real issues"; self-esteem, racial harmony, pregnancy prevention, family
Circulation: 30,000
Distribution: Newsstands; schools/youth centers; homes
Editor: Shannon Berning
Publisher: Alison Amoroso
Cost: $20/yr.; bulk discounts
Sample: $5.00 sample; send check or P.O. or CC# to publisher
Readers' Work Published: Yes, anything

Teen Voices Magazine

is an interactive, educational forum that encourages expression among young women. It honors the sensibilities, ideals, hopes, fears, anger, joy, and insights of teenage girls. *Teen Voices* challenges sexist media images of women and provides an intelligent alternative to gritty, gossipy, fashion-oriented magazines that too often exploit the insecurities of their adolescent audience.

Editorial & Ordering Address:
Women Express, Inc.
316 Huntington Avenue
Boston, MA 02115
617-262-2434
Fax: 617-262-8937

Audience: M/F, ages 12–19
Subject: Youth written: all aspects and interests
Circulation: 165,000
Distribution: Schools (97%); homes (3%)
Editor: Editorial students
Publisher: Stoney McCart
Cost: $25.00/yr. (6 issues)
Sample: SASE (for Canadian requests); $5.00 outside Canada
Readers' Work Published: Exclusively

TG Magazine: Voices of Today's Generation

seeks to empower youth through self-expression in words, art, photography and to allow youth to communicate their ideas to other youth. Its mission is to publish information about emotional growth issues for young people, and it appears in English and French.

Editorial & Ordering Address:
202 Cleveland Street
Toronto, ON
Canada M4S 2W6
416-487-3204

Audience: M/F, ages 8–12
Subject: Science, nature, technology
Circulation: 400,000
Distribution: Homes
Editor: Jonathan Rosenbloom
Publisher: Nina B. Link, Children's Television Workshop
Cost: $16.97/yr. (10 issues)
Sample: $1.75 plus 9" × 12" SASE

3-2-1 Contact

is a science and technology magazine seeking to make readers aware of the science around them. An average issue includes articles on animals and nature, sociology and psychology, and scientists' tasks, with an occasional feature on kid issues such as dealing with divorce in the family. It also contains puzzles and games, math-related activities, fiction, and information on computer programming. The magazine, begun in 1979, has a readers' mail page and publishes children's responses to contests.

Editorial Address:
Children's Television Workshop
One Lincoln Plaza
New York, NY 10023
212-595-3456

Ordering Address:
P.O. Box 51177
Boulder, CO 80322-1177

*Audience: M/F, teenagers—
young adults*
*Subject: Youth issues, youth
services*
Circulation: 200,000
*Distribution: Schools (95%);
other youth organizations
(5%)*
*Editor: Board of 20 youth
editors*
Publisher: Parker Stanzione
*Cost: Free to schools; $10/stu-
dents; $15/others*
*Sample: Send for subscription
information and/or school
profile*
*Readers' Work Published:
All youth writings,
photography*

360° Magazine

is the magazine with every angle, dedicated to providing a forum
for high school students to discuss the issues that directly impact
their lives. Each issue of *360°* takes an in-depth look at a single
social problem as seen through the eyes of teenagers across the
nation. All of the writing, artwork, and photography is created by
young people, for young people. In addition, *360°* interviews
young leaders and profiles innovative programs that are effectively
addressing youth concerns.

Editorial & Ordering Address:
2625 Connecticut Avenue, NW, #400
P.O. Box 25356
Washington, DC 20007
202-628-1836
Fax: 202-628-1843
E-mail: mag360@aol.com

Audience: M/F, grades 4–6
Subject: Current events
Circulation: 1.1 million
Distribution: School (100%)
Editor: Claudia Wallis
Publisher: Lisa Quroz
Cost: $3.95/yr. (26 issues)
*Sample: Call customer service
or write to editorial address*
*Readers' Work Published:
Letters*

Time For Kids

is a weekly classroom news magazine. The goal is to present
current news in an interesting, understandable, and timely
manner. The magazine utilizes the news analysis expertise of Time,
Inc.'s global network of correspondents, writers, and editors.

Editorial Address:
Time, Inc.
1271 Avenue of the Americas
25th Floor
New York, NY 10020
212-522-8738
Fax: 212-522-0372
E-mail: tfk@time.com

Ordering Address:
Time For Kids
Customer Service
P.O. Box 30609
Tampa, FL 33630-0609
800-777-8600
Fax: 800-777-3400

Audience: M/F, ages 8–14
Subject: (Entertainment) folk tales, humorous tales, science, geography, general knowledge
Circulation: 82,000
Distribution: Subscriptions; newsstands; schools; homes
Editor: Anant Pai
Publisher: Anant Pai
Cost: Rs 10/issue; Rs 225/yr.; foreign (air) Rs 720/yr.; foreign (surf) Rs 400/yr.
Sample: Sample copy sent only to schools
Readers' Work Published: Stories, story ideas, jokes accepted from children, then edited, and at times completely rewritten

Tinkle

uses the medium of comics (continuity pictures) to entertain and educate children.

Editorial Address:
India Book House Limited
Fleet Building, MV. Road
Andheri (East)
Bombay 400059, India
850-3981
Fax: 850-0645

Ordering Address:
Rishi Exports
Fleet Building, M.V. Road
Andheri (East)
Bombay 400059, India
850-3158 or 3159

Audience: M/F, ages 15–25
Subject: Current events (political, social, cultural) in the English-speaking world
Circulation: 70,000
Distribution: Subscriptions, newsstands, schools
Editor: Barbara Oudiz
Publisher: Bayard Presse, France
Cost: 30FF or US$6.00/issue

Today in English

a monthly magazine in English for French high school and university students who wish to improve their language skills and learn about events and people in English language countries—Australia, South Africa, Ireland, Canada, the United States, and Great Britain. It reports on political and social issues, profiles, cinema, music, literature, grammar and vocabulary exercises, with full-page color photographs and a vocabulary box on each page for difficult words.

Editorial & Ordering Address:
Today in English
19 rue d'Orleans
92200 Neuilly sur Seine, France
331-41-434885
Fax: 331-41-434898
E-mail: 101372.2635@compuserve.com

Together Time

is designed for 3- and 4-year-olds to take home from church and have their parents read to them as an addition to the Sunday school lesson. Each issue has a story, poem, activity, and letter to the parents. Its purpose is to minister to the young child.

Audience: M/F, ages 3–4
Subject: Sunday school take-home paper
Circulation: 19,000
Distribution: Sunday school classrooms
Editor: Lynda T. Boardman
Publisher: Nazarene Publishing House
Cost: $10.00/yr. (4 issues)
Sample: Free with inquiry and SASE

Editorial Address:
Nazarene Internat'l. Hdqtrs.
   Children's Ministries
6401 The Paseo
Kansas City, MO 64131
816-333-7000, ext. 2347
Fax: 816-333-1683
E-mail: jlstone@nazarene.org

Ordering Address:
Nazarene Publishing House
2923 Troost
Kansas City, MO 64109
800-877-0700

TQ (Teen Quest)

seeks to entertain, encourage, and educate Christian teenagers. The purpose is to show teens why a relationship with Christ is important and how to grow in that relationship. It features teen fiction, Christian music, Christian sports personalities, and other topics and issues important to teens today.

Audience: M/F, ages 13–17
Subject: Christianity
Circulation: 40,000
Distribution: Homes
Editor: Chris Lyon
Publisher: Shepherd Ministries
Cost: $1.95/issue; $14.50/yr. (10 issues)
Sample: Send SASE to editor

Editorial & Ordering Address:
Shepherd Ministries
Box 3512
Irving, TX 75015
214-570-7599
Fax: 214-257-0632

Troll Magazine

provides its readers what they want most—trolls, trolls and more trolls. Regular editorial pieces include troll trivia and history; Gone Trolling, featuring kid and adult troll collections from around the world; Out of Con-Troll, spotlighting trolls making news just about everywhere; Troll Crafts (make your own troll planter!); and games and puzzles galore.

Audience: M/F, ages 6–12
Subject: Trolls
Circulation: 250,000
Distribution: Newsstands, subscriptions
Editor: Liane B. Onish
Publisher: Welsh Publishing Group
Cost: $7.47/yr. (4 issues)
Readers' Work Published: Letters, photographs

Editorial Address:
Marvel Entertainment
   Group, Inc.
87 Park Avenue
New York, NY 10016
212-687-0680
Fax: 212-986-1849

Ordering Address:
P.O. Box 7346
Red Oak, IA 51591
515-243-4543

Audience: M/F, ages 2–5
Subject: General interest, health
Distribution: Homes
Editor: Nancy Axelrad
Publisher: Children's Better Health Institute
Cost: $16.95/yr. (8 issues)
Sample: Teachers and librarians send $1.25 to the editor
Readers' Work Published: Drawings

Turtle Magazine For Preschool Kids

teaches basic concepts of good nutrition and encourages development of learning skills through interactive features. Read-aloud stories and fun activities educate and entertain while providing creative opportunities for family participation. This 36-page illustrated magazine is published 8 times a year.

Editorial Address:
Children's Better Health
　Institute
1100 Waterway Boulevard
P.O. Box 567
Indianapolis, IN 46206
317-636-8881

Ordering Address:
P.O. Box 7133
Red Oak, IA 51591-0133

Audience: M/F, ages 13–18
Subject: Nonfiction, poetry, opinion; reviews incl. book, movie, music; fiction, art, sports
Circulation: 150,000
Distribution: Schools (85%); homes, libraries (15%)
Editor: Stephanie Meyer
Publisher: John Meyer
Cost: $25/yr. (10 issues); $79/yr. (25 copies per month)
Sample: Free on request
Readers' Work Published: Yes, written completely by teens

The 21st Century—Teen Views

is a 40-page newspaper written entirely by teens and for teens. Student-written articles are published in areas as diverse as opinion, fiction, poetry, reviews, community service, art, music, science, sports, and virtually all adolescent issues. The publication seeks to increase self-esteem by providing an opportunity for young adults to develop reading, writing, creative and critical thinking skills, and to read work created by their peers.

Editorial & Ordering Address:
Teen Views
P.O. Box 30
Newton, MA 02161
617-964-6800
E-mail: www.teenpaper.org

Audience: M/F, ages 5–10
Circulation: 250,000
Distribution: Homes, newsstands
Editor: Marta Partington and Steve Charles
Publisher: Children's Better Health Institute
Cost: $21.95/yr. (8 issues)
Sample: $2.50 to editorial address
Readers' Work Published: Art, poetry

U*S* Kids

a 42-page, full-color magazine, allows kids to read about other kids around the country doing unique or interesting things. Fitness and health are emphasized in games and articles. Interactives, puzzles, and games seek to teach learning concepts. The Puzzle Squad features puzzles with a historical focus.

Editorial Address:
Children's Better Health
　Institute
1100 Waterway Boulevard
P.O. Box 567
Indianapolis, IN 46206
317-636-8881
Fax: 317-684-8094

Ordering Address:
P.O. Box 7133
Red Oak, IA 51591-0133

Audience: M, ages 8–12
Subject: Adventure, humor, religion
Circulation: 20,000
Distribution: Homes
Editor: Deborah Christiansen
Publisher: Christian Service Brigade
Cost: $10.00
Sample: $1.85 and 98¢ postage on SASE
Readers' Work Published: Letters, jokes

Venture

speaks to the concerns of boys from a biblical perspective. The diverse needs and interests of boys are addressed in fiction, humor, and religious articles and stories.

Editorial & Ordering Address:
Christian Service Brigade
P.O. Box 150
Wheaton, IL 60189
708-665-0630
Fax: 708-665-0372

Audience: M/F, ages 14–18
Subject: Prose, poetry, fiction, nonfiction, literature, art, photography, drama
Circulation: 3,000
Distribution: Schools (90%); homes (10%)
Editor: Billy C. Clark
Publisher: Longwood College
Cost: $5.50/issue; $9.00/yr. (2 issues) (free copy to Virginia schools)
Sample: Contact Tina Dean at editorial address or phone. Free
Readers' Work Published: Works of VA students and teachers

Virginia Writing

seeks to encourage promising high school writers, artists, and photographers in Virginia by publishing the best prose, poetry, fiction, nonfiction, music, drama, art, and photography submitted to the magazine's editors. Approximately 25 percent of the material published in this 80-page periodical comes from high school teachers.

Editorial & Ordering Address:
Longwood College
201 High Street
Farmville, VA 23909
804-395-2160

Audience: M/F, ages 16–25
Subject: Strategies for college, technical school, and vocational options for Native American youth
Circulation: 100,000
Editor: Georgia Lee Clark
Publisher: Georgia Lee Clark, Communications Publishing Group, Inc.
Cost: $3.00/issue (2 issues/yr.)

Visions

is designed to promote positive images, information, advice, and motivation for Native American youths and young adults. Tips on services suitable to technology and science-minded high school juniors and seniors, discussions of career possibilities, and lists of financial aid sources make up an average issue.

Editorial & Ordering Address:
Communications Publishing Group, Inc.
106 West 11th Street, Suite 250
Kansas City, MO 64105-1806
816-221-4404
Fax: 816-221-1112

Audience: M/F, ages 9–12
Subject: General interest
Editor: Diana Haigwood
*Cost: $5.25/issue; $16.95/yr.
    for 1–9 subscriptions;
    $12.95/yr. for 10–20;
    $9.95/yr. for 21 or more
    (4 issues)*
*Sample: Write or phone to
    request a free sample copy*
*Readers' Work Published:
    Artwork, poetry, essays,
    and creative writing*

Voices of Youth

is a national magazine by, about, and for high school students. The publication is dedicated to acknowledging the ideas and creative work of young people by providing a national forum for student expression.

Editorial & Ordering Address:
P.O. Box 1869
Sonoma, CA 95476
707-938-8314

Audience: M/F, grades 7–12
*Subject: Business, economics,
    English/journalism, math,
    social studies, consumer
    education, careers, voca-
    tional education*
Circulation: 120,000
*Distribution: Schools (99%);
    homes (1%)*
*Editor: Melinda Patterson
    Grenier*
Publisher: Dow Jones & Co.
*Cost: $99.00/semester
    (5 issues); $165.00/yr.
    (9 issues)*
*Sample: Free; call 800-544-
    0522*
*Readers' Work Published:
    Letters, editorials*

The Wall Street Journal Classroom Edition

is a complete newspaper-in-education support program that links textbooks and curriculum to students' lives. It includes a full-color monthly student newspaper, monthly Teacher Guides, a free poster set, and optional videos. The Classroom Edition program brings economic, business, social, and political events into focus and saves teachers' time by packaging high-interest stories with multidisciplinary lesson plans.

Editorial & Ordering Address:
P.O. Box 300
Princeton, NJ 08543
609-520-1295
Fax: 609-520-4299
E-mail: wsjclass@cnj.digex.com
Orders: 800-544-0522

Audience: M/F, ages 12–18
Subject: Weather
Circulation: 13,200
*Distribution: Homes (85%);
    newsstands (15%)*
Editor: Jeff Rosenfeld
*Publisher: Heldref
    Publications*
*Cost: $3.95/issue; $30.00/yr.
    (6 issues)*
Sample: Call 800-365-9753
*Readers' Work Published:
    Letters, occasional articles,
    photos*

Weatherwise

explores the ways the weather helps shape our culture, character, and health. It frequents the pages of our history books, awes us with its power and beauty, and frightens and occasionally kills us. *Weatherwise* shares this experience with its readers through vibrant color photography and crisp, well-written articles.

Editorial & Ordering Address:
Heldref Publications
1319 18th Street NW
Washington, DC 20036
202-296-6267
800-365-9753

Weekly Reader

Audience: M/F, grades preK–6
Subject: News
Distribution: Schools
Editor: Forrest Stone
Publisher: Richard J. LeBrasseur
Cost: Varies by edition, from $2.95 to $4.45/subscription
Sample: Contact Bob Pfister at ordering address

is a graded series of classroom newspapers. The 4- to 8-page weekly provides news, current information, and recreational reading material. Content includes a main news story dealing with a serious contemporary issue and articles on health, science, and safety. Supplements and other extras are included.

Editorial Address:
Weekly Reader Corp.
P.O. Box 2791
Middletown, CT 06457-9291
860-638-2400
Fax: 860-346-5964

Ordering Address:
Subscription Services
Weekly Reader Corp.
3001 Cindel Drive
Delran, NJ 08370
800-446-3355

Western Horseman

Audience: M/F, all ages
Subject: Western horses
Circulation: 230,000
Distribution: Subscriptions, newsstands
Editor: Pat Close
Publisher: Randy Witte
Cost: $2.95/copy in U.S. $20.00/yr. (12 issues)
Sample: Send $5.00 to editorial address
Readers' Work Published: Letters, artwork

features articles dealing with western horse breeds, western history and art, stable and horse management, veterinary care, and coverage of major horse shows and rodeos. The magazine also includes articles about ranch management and western lifestyle.

Editorial & Ordering Address:
P.O. Box 7980
Colorado Springs, CO 80933
719-633-5524

Wild West

Audience: M/F, all ages
Subject: All aspects of the early West
Circulation: 275,000
Distribution: Subscriptions, newsstands
Editor: Greg Lalire
Publisher: Tom O'Keefe
Cost: $22.95/yr. (6 issues)
Samples: $3.95
Readers' Work Published: Only nonfiction articles

covers the American Frontier, from its Eastern beginnings to its Western terminus, featuring articles about the explorers, adventurers, soldiers, settlers, and Indians who are part of our rich Western heritage. This magazine contains carefully researched yet highly readable articles illustrated with rare historical photographs and beautiful art to bring life to the legends of the Wild West.

Editorial Address:
Cowles History Group
741 Miller Drive, SE, #D2
Leesburg, VA 22175-8920
703-779-8302
Fax: 703-779-8345
Orders: 800-829-3340

Wildlife Conservation

Audience: M/F, young adults
Subject: Wildlife conservation, saving wild animals and natural habitats
Circulation: 137,000
Distribution: Newsstands, subscriptions, zoo memberships
Editor: Joan Downs
Publisher: John G. Colson
Cost: $2.95/issue ($3.95 in Canada); $13.95/yr. (6 issues)
Sample: Call circulation department at 718-220-6876–cost of one copy is $2.95 plus $2.00 postage

(formerly called *Animal Kingdom*) invites readers to celebrate the wonders of nature. With these wonders disappearing at an alarming rate, however, the editors believe that everyone must become an active conservationist. Filled with photographs of wild animals and writing by the most distinguished authors in the conservation/nature/science field, *Wildlife Conservation* seeks to be the animal lovers' bible.

Editorial & Ordering Address:
185th Street and Southern Boulevard
Bronx, NY 10460
718-584-2625

Winner

Audience: M/F, grades 4–6
Subject: Drug education
Circulation: 22,000
Distribution: Homes, schools
Editor: Gerald Wheeler
Publisher: The Health Connection
Cost: $8.97/yr. (9 issues)
Sample: Write to ordering address
Readers' Work Published: Artwork, poems, posters on drug education themes

seeks to provide drug education through information, instruction in social skills, role modeling, and positive activities within a framework of stories, articles, games, and puzzles.

Editorial Address:
The Health Connection
55 West Oak Ridge Drive
Hagerstown, MD 21740
301-790-9734

Ordering Address:
P.O. Box 859
Hagerstown, MD 21741
800-548-8700
(outside U.S. 301-790-9735)

With: The Magazine for Radical Christian Youth

Audience: M/F, ages 14–18
Subject: Christian discipleship
Circulation: 6,200
Distribution: Churches (85%); homes (14%); schools (1%)
Editor: Carol Duerksen
Publisher: General Conf. Mennonite Church & Mennonite Church
Cost: $18.95/yr.
Sample: Send 9" × 12" SASE with 5 first-class stamps

is published for high-school-age youth in the U.S. and Canada. Most readers attend Mennonite or Brethren Churches. *With* seeks to help Christian youth in their spiritual growth and to show non-Christian youth the difference Christian faith could make in their lives.

Editorial & Ordering Address:
General Conference Mennonite Church & Mennonite Church
P.O. Box 347
Newton, KS 67114
316-283-5100

Audience: M/F, ages 13 and up
Subject: Sailing, building, models, knots, beginning boat building
Circulation: 104,000
Distribution: Homes (60%); newsstands (40%)
Editor: Matthew Murphy
Publisher: Carl Cramer
Cost: $4.99/issue; $27.95/yr.
Sample: Free copy, write to Rick Wasowicz at publication address

WoodenBoat Magazine

is the bimonthly magazine for wooden boat owners, builders, and designers, professional and amateur alike. The magazine works to convey quality, integrity, and involvement in the creation and care of the craft, to entertain, to inform, to inspire, and to provide readers—young and old—with access to individuals who are deeply experienced in the world of boats.

Editorial & Ordering Address:
WoodenBoat Publications, Inc.
P.O. Box 78
Brooklin, ME 04616
207-359-4651
Fax: 207-359-8920

Audience: M/F, grades K–8
Subject: Creative writing, art by and for children
Distribution: Homes (30%); schools (60%); newsstands (10%)
Editor: Stuart Ungar
Publisher: Playful Productions, Inc.
Cost: $4.95/issue; $18.00/yr. (4 issues)
Sample: Write and include a check for $4.95
Readers' Work Published: Letters, poetry, short stories; special consideration given to unique group projects and work from mentally and physically challenged youths

Word Dance Magazine

was established to give today's youth a quality forum for creative expression. It seeks to inform and inspire young people by providing a vehicle that is uniquely theirs with the intent of gaining greater popular support and to contribute to giving the young a lively, thorough, and truthful education.

Editorial & Ordering Address:
P.O. Box 10804
Wilmington, DE 19850
302-328-6834

Audience: M/F, all ages
Subject: Woodworking and home improvement
Circulation: 860,000
Editor: Christopher Inman
Publisher: Donald B. Peschke
Cost: $3.95/issue; $14.95/yr. (6 issues)
Sample: Send SASE

Workbench

is a how-to magazine that gives step-by-step instructions for a variety of woodworking and home improvement projects for do-it-yourselfers of all skill levels.

Editorial Address:
August Home Publishing
2200 Grand Avenue
Des Moines, IA 50312
515-282-7000

Ordering Address:
P.O. Box 842
Des Moines, IA 50304
800-311-3991

Audience: M/F, ages 14–18
Subject: Environmental, social, and consumer problems
Editor: Kathy Cone Newton
Publisher: Southwest Research and Information Center
Cost: $3.50/issue; $12.00/yr.; $8.50/students or retired (4 issues)

The Workbook

is in its 18th year of publication. Each 50-page issue carries an authoritative feature article on an environmental issue, along with a regular "Sources of Information" section, generally 30 pages of reviews of books and other publications by small and alternative presses. The reviews cover more than 25 categories of environmental and social issues.

Editorial & Ordering Address:
105 Stanford SE
P.O. Box 4524
Albuquerque, NM 97106
505-262-1862
Fax: 505-262-1864

Audience: M/F, grades 5–12
Subject: World news and geography
Distribution: Schools
Editor: Alan Lenhoff
Publisher: Richard J. LeBrasseur, Weekly Reader Corporation
Cost: $79.95 classroom set

World Newsmap of the Week/Headline Focus

is a current events program that includes up-to-the-minute news summaries, full-color world maps, background information, graphics, and teaching suggestions. Now in its 56th year, *World Newsmap of the Week* is published every week of the school year.

Editorial Address:
Weekly Reader Corp.
P.O. Box 2791
Middletown, CT 06457-9291
806-638-2400
Fax: 806-346-5964

Ordering Address:
Weekly Reader Corp.
3001 Cindel Drive
Delran, NJ 08370
800-446-3355

Audience: M/F, grades 7–12
Subject: English, journalism
Circulation: 165,328
Distribution: Schools
Editor: Carol Elliott
Publisher: Richard J. LeBrasseur
Cost: $7.95/subscription for 15 or more
Readers' Work Published: Book reviews, journal entries, writing contests: essay, editorial, fiction

Writing!

seeks to motivate students to write. Focus articles address a writing problem or challenge. *Writing!* includes practical writing exercises, examples of student writing, and interviews with successful authors. New columns are a monthly vocabulary building section and a review of significant works of fiction or nonfiction accessible to young adult readers.

Editorial Address:
Weekly Reader Corp.
P.O. Box 2791
Middletown, CT 06457-9291
806-638-2400
Fax: 806-346-5964

Ordering Address:
Weekly Reader Corp.
3001 Cindel Drive
Delran, NJ 08370
800-446-3355

YES Magazine

is the only magazine to focus on youth achievers in urban schools. The distinctive journalistic style covers the scholastic and personal achievements of students nationwide, as well as offering useful information and resources to help young people succeed both in and out of the classroom. *YES* educates and entertains with a wide range of topics including tips on college and careers, health and fitness, and news about the environment.

Audience: M/F, ages 12–18 urban school youth
Subject: Peer role models, how-to, music, money management, scholarship information
Circulation: 100,000
Distribution: Schools
Editor: Jan M. Edgenton Johnson
Publisher: Henry C. Johnson
Cost: $15.00/school yr. (10 issues)
Sample: Write for sample copy
Readers' Work Published: Yes

Editorial & Ordering Address:
YES Communications Inc.
144 North Avenue
Plainfield, NJ 07060
908-754-4466
Fax: 908-753-1036

YM Magazine (Young & Modern)

gives its young female readers what they can't get anywhere else: crucial information on the subjects they care about most—dating, friendships, self-esteem, love, beauty, fashion, celebrities, pop culture, career, and college life. *YM* provides the facts that young women need to know in order to live smart, confident, and safe lives, all in a fun, provocative format.

Audience: F, ages 12–17
Subject: Relationships, fashion, beauty, health and fitness, entertainment and celebrities, job and college advice
Circulation: 2 million
Distribution: Subscriptions (63%); newsstands (37%)
Editor: Sally Lee
Publisher: Victoria Lasdon Rose
Cost: $2.95/issue; $13.97/yr.
Sample: On newsstand
Readers' Work Published: First person stories, true stories of embarrassing moments, occasional special features, letters

Editorial Address:
Gruner & Jahr Publishing
685 Third Avenue
New York, NY 10017
212-878-8700

Ordering Address:
YM
P.O. Box 3060
Harlan, IA 51593-2124

Young Judaean

is the magazine for younger members of Young Judaea, the Zionist youth movement. *Young Judaean* attempts to educate and inform youth between grades 2 and 8 on a range of Jewish topics and provide a forum for the members of Young Judaea on Zionism, Judaism, America, Israel, youth, and current events.

Audience: M/F, ages 8–13
Subject: Israel and Jewish life
Circulation: 5,000
Distribution: Homes
Editor: Linda K. Shaffzin
Publisher: Hadassah Zionist Youth Commission
Cost: $5.00/yr. (4 issues)
Sample: Send requests to editorial address with SASE and $2.00

Editorial Address:
Schaffzin & Schaffzin
P.O. Box 173
Merion Station, PA 19066
215-642-8389
Fax: 215-642-8070

Ordering Address:
c/o Hadassah Zionist
Youth Commission
50 W. 58th Street
New York, NY 10019

Young Salvationist

is published for high school age members of the Salvation Army. All material is from an evangelical world view.

Editorial & Ordering Address:
The Salvation Army
P.O. Box 269
Alexandria, VA 22313
703-684-5539
Fax: 703-684-5500

Audience: M/F, high school
Subject: Articles of interest to teens
Circulation: 50,000
Distribution: Free distribution (95%); subscriptions (5%)
Editor: Lesa Davis, Production Manager
Publisher: The Salvation Army
Cost: $4.00/yr.
Sample: 9" × 12" SASE with 3 U.S. 1st class stamps

Young Scholar

seeks to reach teenagers who care about education and about success. The editorial content is designed to give readers ideas for and perspectives on success and achieving goals. The magazine focuses on issues that affect high-performance teenagers both inside and outside the classroom.

Editorial & Ordering Address:
Scholar Communications, Inc.
4905 Pine Cone Drive, Suite 1
Durham, NC 27707
919-489-1916
Fax: 919-489-4767
E-mail: gsanders@interpath.com

Audience: M/F, ages 14–18
Subject: Lifestyle for high-performance students
Circulation: Debuted in October 1993—immediate goal is 25,000
Distribution: Subscriptions
Editor: Greg M. Sanders
Publisher: Webb C. Howell, Scholar Communications
Cost: $2.75/issue; $14.97/yr. (6 issues)
Sample: Free, include SASE (digest-size) with 4 stamps
Readers' Work Published: Viewpoints

Young Voices

features stories, essays, drawings, and poems by elementary through high school-age people, who are paid for their contributions. *Young Voices* is for anyone interested in the perspective of young people.

Editorial & Ordering Address:
P.O. Box 2321
Olympia, WA 98507
206-357-4683

Audience: M/F, all ages
Subject: Stories, poems, essays, drawings by young people
Circulation: 2,000
Distribution: Homes (40%); schools (20%); newsstands (40%)
Publisher: Steve Charak
Cost: $3.00/issue; $15.00/yr. (6 issues)
Sample: Send $4.00
Readers' Work Published: Exclusively

The Youngster

published by the Society of St. Paul, seeks to promote Christian values to develop human personality and to educate children. Based on the belief that children need Christian and human formation, *The Youngster* attempts to encourage children to ask questions, interviews children about social issues, gives reflections on the gospel and illustrates gospel values in comics, explores issues about teen life, and holds yearly contests. Readers' poems, letters, and contest answers are published. This 36-page, 4-color, monthly magazine first appeared in June 1955.

Audience: M/F, ages 10–14
Subject: Christian formation and personality development
Circulation: 45,000
Distribution: Homes; schools/classrooms; newsstands; distribution centers
Editor: Bro. Hansel B. Mapayo, SSP
Publisher: Society of St. Paul
Cost: $10/issue; $100/10 months
Sample: Contact Rey Naranja at editorial number (loc 215) for sample issue (free)
Readers' Work Published: Drawings, poems, prayers, and letters

Editorial & Ordering Address:
The Youngster
7708 St. Paul Road/SAU Makati
Metro, Manila 1203, Philippines
895-9701 to 04
Fax: 632-817-8955

Youpi

helps children discover for themselves the world and all its mysteries: wildlife, nature, objects, and professions. With *Youpi*, children learn to play with words and discover new ones. Every month, in the middle of the magazine, there's a big booklet on an important topic—prehistoric man, wildlife of the savanna, building a house, or Christmas legends.

Audience: M/F, ages 3–7
Subject: General knowledge
Circulation: 49,261
Distribution: Homes, newsstands, schools
Editor: Agnés Rochefort Turquin
Publisher: Bayard Presse
Cost: 29 FF/issue; 299 FF/yr.

Editorial Address:
Bayard Presse
3 rue Bayard
Paris 75008, France
331-44-356060
Fax: 331-44-35604

Ordering Address:
Bayard Presse International
BP 12
99505 Paris Entreprise France
331-44-216000
Fax: 331-20-274192

Your Big Backyard

brings a conservation message to preschoolers by focusing on animals and nature. Each issue includes a special "read-to-me" story often including the adventures of the magazine's mascot. This periodical encourages language arts skills and number and color identification for 3- to 6-year-old children.

Audience: M/F, ages 3–6
Subject: Nature and conservation
Circulation: 500,000
Distribution: Homes
Editor: Kathy Walsh
Publisher: National Wildlife Federation
Cost: $12.00/yr. (12 issues)
Sample: Contact editor

Editorial & Ordering Address:
National Wildlife Federation
8925 Leesburg Pike
Vienna, VA 22184
703-790-4000
Orders: 800-432-6564

Youth 96

Audience: M/F, ages 13–18
Subject: Christian general interest
Circulation: 414,000
Distribution: Homes (60%); libraries, waiting rooms (40%)
Editor: Mike Bennett
Publisher: Worldwide Church of God
Cost: One-year free subscription (6 issues)
Sample: Free on request
Readers' Work Published: Letters, poems, advice, photos, teen fiction

a general interest magazine for Christian teens, seeks to help readers deal with real-life concerns about the future, personal and family problems, popularity, looks, fears, friendships, success, sexuality, emotions, and much more. Four-color graphics help make relevant biblical principles come alive.

Editorial & Ordering Address:
Worldwide Church of God
300 W. Green Street
Pasadena, CA 91123
818-304-6077
Fax: 818-795-0107

Youth Update

Audience: M/F, ages 14–18
Subject: Application of Catholic principles to timely topics
Circulation: 23,000
Distribution: Homes, schools, parishes
Editor: Carol Ann Morrow
Publisher: St. Anthony Messenger Press
Cost: $12.00/yr. (12 issues)
Sample: Business-size SASE

seeks to support the growth of teenagers in a life of faith through focus on a single topic per edition. The newsletter offers examples, strategies, and pertinent church teachings on the topic. Topics range from popularity to sacraments to volunteer work.

Editorial & Ordering Address:
St. Anthony Messenger Press
1615 Republic Street
Indianapolis, IN 46219
513-241-5615
Fax: 513-241-0399

Zelos

Audience: M/F, ages 15–22
Subject: Christian living
Distribution: Churches, subscriptions
Editor: Amy Cox
Publisher: Scripture Press Publications, Inc.
Cost: $8.75/yr.
Sample: Send SASE to editor
Readers' Work Published: True stories, poetry

is a Christian lifestyle notebook to help high school students grow in their daily relationship with God. True stories–personal experience and as-told-to profiles and interviews about everyday teens or celebrities with strong Christian testimonies are presented. *Zelos* looks for fresh, motivating, hard-hitting stories to challenge its readers. All materials must have a clear Christian perspective and be realistic. Resolutions should be natural, and characters and subjects should not be too good to be true.

Editorial & Ordering Address:
Scripture Press Publications, Inc.
4050 Lee Vance View
Colorado Springs, CO 80918
800-708-5550
Fax: 800-323-7543

Audience: M/F, ages 8–14
Subject: Consumer education
Circulation: 350,000
Distribution: Homes (80%); schools (20%)
Editor: Charlotte M. Baecher
Publisher: Consumers Union of the U.S.
Cost: $16.00/yr. (6 issues)

Zillions: The Consumer Reports for Kids

is intended to help 8- to 14-year-olds cope with the increasingly complex world of the 1990s. The magazine evaluates products (toys, sports equipment, video games, etc.) and advertising; explores earning/saving/money-management skills; promotes informed decision making.

Editorial Address:
Consumers Union
101 Truman Avenue
Yonkers, NY 10703-1057
914-378-2551

Ordering Address:
Zillions Subscription Dept.
P.O. Box 51777
Boulder, CO 80321-1777
800-234-2078

Audience: M/F, ages 7–14
Subject: Sciences, humanities, kid accomplishment
Circulation: 32,321
Distribution: Subscriptions (35%); bulk sales (40%); nonprofit education outreach (25%)
Editor: Dr. Kevin T. Jones
Publisher: The ZiNj Education Project
Cost: $2.95/issue; $1.50/issue for bulk orders (+S&H)
Sample: $2.95 each
Readers' Work Published: ZiNj is written by kids and scientists; articles, book reviews, questions for Dr. What, artwork, activities and photos are accepted

ZiNj Magazine

is a hero-sized, scholastically hip publication that involves kids in exploring the world using "Dinosaurs, Fossils, Ancient People and Other Really Cool Old Stuff" as a starting point. *ZiNj* launches kids into an interdisciplinary exploration of the sciences and humanities by encouraging investigation, and by supporting kids in tackling challenging information. *ZiNj Magazine* is written by kids, for kids with help from top-notch scientists.

Editorial & Ordering Address:
The ZiNj Education Project
300 Rio Grande
Salt Lake City, UT 84101
801-533-3565
Fax: 801-533-3503

Audience: M/F, ages 5–14
Subject: Wildlife
Circulation: 350,000
Distribution: Homes
Editor: Marjorie McGuire
Publisher: Allen Greer
Cost: $20.95/subscription (10 issues)

Zoobooks

is designed to be an entertaining and informative full-color wildlife series published in collectible monthly "books." Each issue contains photographs, artwork, and scientifically accurate facts about the world's wildlife and generally covers a specific animal or group of animals.

Editorial & Ordering Address:
Wildlife Education Limited
9820 Willow Creek Rd.
Suite 300
San Diego, CA 92131
619-578-2440
Fax: 619-578-9658

These indexes are designed to help you identify publications that meet specific age ranges and interests.

Magazines listed in the guide are arranged alphabetically by title. They are divided into four age groups: ages 0 to 6 years, ages 6 to 11 years, ages 8 to 14 years, and ages 14 years and up, roughly corresponding to reading level. Many magazines are suitable for readers of a wider range of reading levels and have been listed in several age groups.

The second index identifies 36 areas of interest and lists magazines addressing them. Again, many publications cross over interest lines and are listed in several categories.

Magazines that accept readers' work are grouped as those publishing readers' work (1) exclusively, (2) regularly, and (3) occasionally.

The last index lists alphabetically the kids' magazines followed by the teens' magazines.

Ages 0–6

Babar
Babybug
Coulicou
Crayola Kids
Fantastic Flyer
Happy Times
Highlights for Children
Humpty Dumpty
La Giostra (The Merry-Go-
    Round)
Ladybug, The Magazine for
    Young Children
Learningland

Les Belles Histoires
    (Beautiful Stories)
Let's Find Out
Pomme D'Api
Popi
Sesame Street Magazine
Shoofly: An Audiomagazine
    for Children
Story Mates
Together Time
Turtle Magazine for
    Preschool Kids
Youpi
Your Big Backyard

Ages 6–11

ABC
Acorn, The
American Girl
Astrapi
Babar
Barbie, The Magazine for
    Girls
Black Belt for Kids
Boodle
Boomerang! A Children's
    Audio Magazine About
    Big Ideas
Boys' Life
Brilliant Star
Casper the Friendly Ghost
Chickadee
Child Life
Children's Magazine
Children's Playmate
Children's World
Clavier's Piano Explorer
Coulicou
Counselor
Crayola Kids
Creative Kids
Creative with Words
    Publications (CWW)
Current Health I
Daybreak Star Indian Reader
Disney Adventures
Dolphin Log
EarthSavers

Eos
Fantastic Flyer
Flohkiste (Fleabag) Grade 1
Girls' Life
Goldfinch, The
Guideposts for Kids
Harambee
Hibou
High Adventure
Highlights for Children
HiP Magazine
Home Altar, The
Hopscotch: The Magazine
    for Girls
InSights Magazine
J'Aime Lire
Jack and Jill
Keys for Kids
Kid City
Kids Discover
Kids for Saving Earth News
KIND News (KIND—Kids
    In Nature's Defense)
Koala Club News
Koululainen (Schoolchild)
La Giostra (The Merry-Go-
    Round)
Lad
Ladybug, The Magazine for
    Young Children
Les Belles Histoires
    (Beautiful Stories)

Ages 8–14 cont'd.

EarthSavers
El Sol
Eos
Faces
Falcon Magazine
Girls' Life
Goldfinch, The
Grain De Soleil
Guide Magazine
Guideposts for Kids
Harambee
Hibou
High Adventure
HiP Magazine
Hopscotch: The Magazine for Girls
Images Doc
In 2 Print
InSights Magazine
Je Bouquine
Junior Scholastic
Junior Trails
Kids Discover
Kids for Saving Earth News
Kids Today
Kids Today Mini-Magazine
Know Your World Extra
Koala Club News
Koululainen (Schoolchild)
Malihai Clubs Newsletter, The
Merlyn's Pen: The National Magazine of Student Writing—Middle School Edition Grades 6–9
MetroKids
Monkeyshines
My Friend: The Catholic Magazine for Kids
Nandan
National Geographic World
New Moon: The Magazine for Girls and Their Dreams
Nickelodeon Magazine
Nineteenth Avenue
Nipitiri
Norsk Barneblad
Odyssey

On the Line
Otterwise: For Kids Who Are into Saving Animals and the Environment
Owl Magazine
Plays: The Drama Magazine for Young People
Pockets
Points De Repére
R-A-D-A-R
Racing for Kids
Rainbow
Ranger Rick
react
READ Magazine
Scholastic Choices
Scholastic Math
School Magazine
School Mates
Science Weekly
Scott Stamp Monthly
Seedling Series: Short Story International
Shofar
Signatures from Big Sky
Skipper
Skipping Stones: A Multicultural Children's Quarterly
Soccer JR.
Sports Illustrated for Kids
Stone Soup: The Magazine by Young Writers and Artists
Superman and Batman Magazine
Surprises: Activities for Today's Kids and Parents
Taghna T-tfal
Tapori
Teen Beat
Teen Power
3-2-1 Contact
Time for Kids
Tinkle
Troll Magazine
Venture
Western Horseman

Age Index

Subject Index

Subject Index

Family Values cont'd.

Freeway
Grain De Soleil
Guide Magazine
Guideposts for Kids
Happy Times
High Adventure
Home Altar, The
I. D. (Senior High)
Junior Trails
Keys for Kids
Kol ha'T'nua
Lad

Magazine for Christian
  Youth!, The
Nandan
New Era Magazine
R-A-D-A-R
Story Mates
Straight Magazine
With: The Magazine for
  Radical Christian Youth
Youth Update
Zelos

Fine & Performing Arts, Music

Clavier's Piano Explorer
Dramatics
Hit Parader
Images Doc

In 2 Print
Plays, The Drama Magazine
  for Young People
Scholastic Art

Foreign Culture

Aerostato (Balloon)
Æskan (The Youth)
Ahora
Aktuell
Allons-y!
Beijing Review
Bonjour
Ca Va?
Champs-Elysees
Chez Nous

Claudia
Das Rad
El Sol
Faces
I Love English
J'Aime Lire
Je Bouquine
¿Que Tal?
Schuss
Today in English

Foreign Language

Ahora
Aktuell
Allons-y!
Bonjour
Ca Va?
Champs-Elysees
Chez Nous

Claudia
Das Rad
El Sol
I Love English
Phosphore
¿Que Tal?
Schuss

General Interest

Acorn, The
Æskan (The Youth)
Alateen Talk
American Girl
Astrapi
Barbie, The Magazine for
  Girls

Boys' Life
Cavall Fort
Child Life
Children's Digest
Children's Magazine

Hobby

American Craft
Autoweek
Balls & Strikes
Boys' Life
Canoe Magazine
Chess Life
Coins Magazine
FFA New Horizons
FineScale Modeler
Girls' Life
Hopscotch: The Magazine for Girls
InSights Magazine

Karate/Kung Fu Illustrated
Model Railroader
Racing For Kids
Radio Control Car Action
Sail
School Mates
Scott Stamp Monthly
Slap Magazine
Soccer JR.
Surfer
WoodenBoat
Workbench

Language Arts

Babar
Babybug
Boodle
ByLine
Children's World
Claremont Review, The
Crayola Kids
Creative Kids
Creative with Words Publications (CWW)
Cricket Magazine
Dialogue: A World of Ideas for Visually Impaired People of All Ages
Edge: The High Performance Electronic Magazine for Students
Goldfinch, The
Highlights for Children
In 2 Print
J'Aime Lire
Je Bouquine
Kid City
Know Your World Extra
La Giostra (The Merry-Go-Round)
Ladybug, The Magazine for Young Children
Learningland
Les Belles Histoires (Beautiful Stories)
Merlyn's Pen Senior Edition: Grades 9–12

Merlyn's Pen: The National Magazine of Student Writing—Middle School Edition Grades 6–9
New Moon Magazine
READ Magazine
Scholastic Scope
Scholastic Sprint
School Magazine
Seedling Series: Short Story International
Shoofly: An Audiomagazine for Children
Signatures from Big Sky
Skipping Stones: A Multicultural Children's Quarterly
Spider
Stone Soup, The Magazine by Young Writers and Artists
Storyworks
Student Series: Short Story International
Surprises: Activities for Today's Kids and Parents
TG Magazine: Voices of Today's Generation
360° Magazine
21st Century-Teen Views, The
Virginia Writing
Word Dance
Writing!
ZiNj Magazine

Literature

Babybug
Children's World
Claremont Review, The
Creative with Words
  Publications (CWW)
Cricket Magazine
Dialogue: A World of Ideas
  for Visually Impaired
  People of All Ages
Edge: The High Performance
  Electronic Magazine for
  Students
Faces
Hobson's Choice: Science
  Fiction & Technology
In 2 Print
J'Aime Lire
Ladybug, The Magazine for
  Young Children
Literary Cavalcade
Merlyn's Pen Senior Edition:

Grades 9–12
Merlyn's Pen: The National
  Magazine of Student
  Writing—Middle School
  Edition Grades 6–9
School Magazine
Seedling Series: Short Story
  International
Shoofly: An Audiomagazine
  for Children
Signatures From Big Sky
Spider
Stone Soup: The Magazine
  by Young Writers and
  Artists
Storyworks
Student Series: Short Story
  International
Virginia Writing
Word Dance
Writing!

Math

Quantum
Scholastic Dynamath
Scholastic Math

Surprises: Activities for
  Today's Kids and Parents

Multiculturalism

AIM— America's
  Intercultural Magazine
Daybreak Star Indian Reader
Harambee
How on Earth!: Youth
  Supporting
  Compassionate,
  Ecologically Sound Living
Nandan

Points De Repére
¿Que Tal?
Schuss
Skipping Stones: A
  Multicultural Children's
  Quarterly
Tapori
Teen Voices Magazine

Nature

Astrapi
Canoe Magazine
Chickadee
Colorado Kids
Coulicou
Dolphin Log
Falcon Magazine
Hibou

Hopscotch: The Magazine
  for Girls
Kids Discover
Kids for Saving Earth News
KIND News (KIND—Kids
  In Nature's Defense)
Malihai Clubs Newsletter,
  The

Subject Index

Religion cont'd.

Young Judaean
Youngster, The
Youth 96

Youth Update
Zelos

Science

Astrapi
Chem Matters
Chickadee
Current Science
Dolphin Log
Highlights for Children
Hopscotch: The Magazine
  for Girls
Images Doc
Kid City
Kids Discover
Monkeyshines
National Geographic World
Odyssey
Owl Magazine

Science News: The Weekly
  Newsmagazine of Science
Science Weekly
Science World
Scienceland
Spaceflight: The International
  Magazine of Space and
  Astronautics
SuperScience Blue Edition
SuperScience Red
Surprises, Activities for
  Today's Kids and Parents
3-2-1 Contact
Weatherwise
ZiNj Magazine

Social Studies

Faces
Junior Scholastic
Know Your World Extra
Scholastic Update

Sky & Telescope
Surprises: Activities for
  Today's Kids and Parents
Time for Kids

Sports

Ahora
Aktuell
Allons-y!
AutoWeek
Balls & Strikes
Black Belt for Kids
Bonjour
Boys' Life
Ca Va?
Canoe Magazine
Chez Nous
Claudia
Colorado Kids
Das Rad
Dialogue: A World of Ideas
  for Visually Impaired
  People of All Ages

El Sol
Girls' Life
Hopscotch: The Magazine
  for Girls
I Love English
InSights Magazine
Karate/Kung Fu Illustrated
Racing for Kids
react
Sail
Soccer JR.
Sports Illustrated for Kids
Surfer

Exclusive Use of Readers' Work

How on Earth!: Youth Supporting Compassionate, Ecologically Sound Living
In 2 Print
Merlyn's Pen Senior Edition: Grades 9–12
Merlyn's Pen: The National Magazine of Student Writing—Middle School Edition Grades 6–9

New Moon Magazine
Stone Soup: The Magazine by Children
TG Magazine: Voices of Today's Generation
360º Magazine
21st Century–Teen Views, The
Virginia Writing
Young Voices

Regular Use of Readers' Work

Acorn, The
Æskan (The Youth)
Alateen Talk
American Careers
Black Belt for Kids
Blue Jean Magazine: For Teen Girls Who Dare
Boodle
Boomerang! A Children's Audio Magazine About Big Ideas
Brilliant Star
California Weekly Explorer
Campus Life
Cavall Fort
Child Life
Circle K
Claremont Review, The
Creative Kids
Creative with Words Publications (CWW)
Daybreak Star Indian Reader
Devo'Zine
Edge: The high performance electronic magazine for students
Falcon Magazine
FFA New Horizons
For Graduates Only
For Seniors Only
Girls' Life
Goldfinch, The
Highlights for Children
Jack and Jill
Junior Scholastic

Keynoter
KIND News (KIND—Kids In Nature's Defense)
Koala Club News
Kol Ha T'nua
Koululainen
Literary Cavalcade
Magazine for Christian Youth!, The
MetroKids
Nandan
New Era Magazine
Nipitiri
Norsk Barneblad
Olomeinu/Our World
On the Line
Otterwise: For Kids Who Are into Saving Animals and the Environment
Pockets
Racing For Kids
react
Scholastic Art
Scholastic Dynmath
Scholastic Math
School Mates
Signatures from Big Sky
Skipper
Skipping Stones: A Multicultural Children's Quarterly
Soccer JR.
Storyworks
Straight Magazine
Taghna T-tfal

**Regular Use of
Readers' Work
cont'd.**

Tapori
'Teen Magazine
Teen Power
Teen Times
Teen Voices Magazine
Tinkle
Voices of Youth
Word Dance

Writing!
Yes Magazine
YM (Young and Modern)
Young Scholar
Youth 96
Zelos
ZiNj Magazine

**Occasional Use of
Readers' Work**

Aerostato (Balloon)
Ahora
AIM–America's Intercultural
    Magazine
Aktuell
Allons-y!
American Girl
Balls & Strikes
Barbie, The Magazine for
    Girls
Beijing Review
Bonjour
Bread for God's Children
ByLine
Ca Va?
Calliope
Casper the Friendly Ghost
Chess Life
Chez Nous
Chickadee
Children's Digest
Children's Magazine
Children's Playmate
Children's World
Cobblestone
Coins Magazine
Coulicou
Crayola Kids
Das Rad
Disney Adventures
Dramatics
EarthSavers
El Sol
Eos
Faces
Fantastic Flyer
Field & Stream, Jr.
Guide Magazine

Harambee
Hibou
HiP Magazine
Hit Parader
Hopscotch: The Magazine
    for Girls
Humpty Dumpty
Hype Hair
InSights Magazine
Karate/Kung Fu Illustrated
Kids for Saving Earth News
Kids Today
La Giostra (The Merry-Go-
    Round)
Lad
My Friend, The Catholic
    Magazine For Kids
National Geographic World
Nickelodeon Magazine
Nineteenth Avenue
Odyssey
Owl Magazine
¿Que Tal?
R-A-D-A-R
Radio Control Car Action
Ranger Rick
Scholastic Action Magazine
School Magazine
Schuss
Shofar
Shoofly: An Audiomagazine
    for Children
Slap Magazine
Sports Illustrated for Kids
Superman and Batman
    Magazine
SuperScience Red

**Occasional Use of
Readers' Work
cont'd.**

Surprises, Activities for
   Today's Kids and Parents
Teen Beat
Troll Magazine
U*S* Kids
Venture
Wall Street Journal
   Classroom Edition, The

Weatherwise
Western Horseman
Winner
With: The Magazine for
   Radical Christian Youth
Workbench
Youngster, The

ABC
Acorn, The
American Girl
Astrapi
Babar
Babybug
Barbie, The Magazine for Girls
Black Belt for Kids
Boodle
Boomerang! A Children's Audio Magazine About Big Ideas
Boys' Life
Brilliant Star
California Weekly Explorer
Calliope
Casper the Friendly Ghost
Cavall Fort
Chickadee
Child Life
Children's Digest
Children's Magazine
Children's Playmate
Children's World
Clavier's Piano Explorer
Cobblestone
Colorado Kids
Coulicou
Counselor
Cracked
Crayola Kids
Creative Kids
Creative with Words Publications (CWW)
Cricket Magazine
Crusader Magazine
Current Health I
Daybreak Star Indian Reader
Disney Adventures
Dolphin Log
EarthSavers
Eos
Faces
Falcon Magazine
Fantastic Flyer
Flohkiste (Fleabag) Grade 1
Girls' Life

Goldfinch, The
Grain De Soleil
Guide Magazine
Guideposts for Kids
Happy Times
Harambee
Hibou
High Adventure
Highlights for Children
HiP Magazine
Home Altar, The
Hopscotch: The Magazine for Girls
Humpty Dumpty
Images Doc
InSights Magazine
J'Aime Lire
Jack and Jill
Je Bouquine
Junior Scholastic
Junior Trails
Keys for Kids
Kid City
Kids Discover
Kids for Saving Earth News
Kids Today
Kids Today Mini-Magazine
KIND News (KIND—Kids In Nature's Defense)
Know Your World Extra
Koala Club News
Koululainen (Schoolchild)
La Giostra (The Merry-Go-Round)
Lad
Ladybug, The Magazine for Young Children
Learningland
Les Belles Histoires (Beautiful Stories)
Let's Find Out
Merlyn's Pen: The National Magazine of Student Writing—Middle School Edition Grades 6–9
MetroKids
Mini Page
Monkeyshines

My Friend, The Catholic Magazine for Kids
Nandan
National Geographic World
New Moon Magazine
Nickelodeon Magazine
Nineteenth Avenue
Nipitiri
Norsk Barneblad
Odyssey
Olomeinu/Our World
On the Line
Otterwise: For Kids Who Are into Saving Animals and the Environment
Owl Magazine
Plays, The Drama Magazine for Young People
Pockets
Points De Repére
Pomme D'Api
Popi
R-A-D-A-R
Racing for Kids
Rainbow
Ranger Rick
READ Magazine
Scholastic Dynamath
Scholastic Math
Scholastic News
Scholastic Sprint
School Magazine
School Mates
Science Weekly
Scienceland
Seedling Series: Short Story International
Sesame Street Magazine
Shofar
Shoofly: An Audiomagazine for Children
Signatures from Big Sky
Skipping Stones: A Multicultural Children's Quarterly
Soccer JR.
Spider: The Magazine for Children

Sports Illustrated for Kids
Stone Soup: The Magazine
  by Young Writers and
  Artists
Story Mates
Storyworks
Superman and Batman
  Magazine
SuperScience Blue Edition
SuperScience Red
Surprises: Activities for
  Today's Kids and Parents

Taghna T-tfal
Tapori
3-2-1 Contact
Time for Kids
Tinkle
Together Time
Troll Magazine
Turtle Magazine for
  Preschool Kids
U*S* Kids
Venture
Weekly Reader

Winner
Word Dance
World Newsmap of the
  Week/Headline Focus
Young Judaean
Youngster, The
Youpi
Your Big Backyard
Zillions: The Consumer
  Reports for Kids
ZiNj Magazine
Zoobooks

Abrams Planetarium Sky
  Calender
Aerostato (Balloon)
Æskan (The Youth)
Ahora
AIM—America's
  Intercultural Magazine
Aktuell
Alateen Talk
Allons-y!
American Careers Magazine
American Craft
Animals
AutoWeek
Balls & Strikes
Beijing Review
Black Collegian, The
Blue Jean Magazine: For
  Teen Girls Who Dare
Bonjour
Bread for God's Children
ByLine
Ca Va?
Campus Life
Canada and the World
Canoe Magazine
Career World
Careers & Colleges
Challenge
Champs-Elyseés
Chem Matters
Chess Life
Chez Nous
Circle K
Claremont Review, The
Claudia
Coins Magazine
College Bound
College PreView
Conqueror, The
Current Events
Current Health II
Current Science
Das Rad
Devo'Zine
Dialogue: A World of Ideas
  for Visually Impaired
  People of All Ages
Dramatics
Edge: The High Performance
  Electronic Magazine for

Students
El Sol
FFA New Horizons
FineScale Modeler
First Opportunity
For Graduates Only
For Seniors Only
Freeway
G-Geschichte mit Pfiff
  (History with Pizazz)
Hit Parader
Hobson's Choice: Science
  Fiction & Technology
How on Earth!: Youth
  Supporting Compassionate,
  Ecologically Sound Living
Hype Hair
I Love English
I. D. (Senior High)
In 2 Print
In Motion
Journal of the West
Karate/Kung Fu Illustrated
Keynoter
Kol ha'T'nua
Lefthander Magazine
Literary Cavalcade
Magazine for Christian
  Youth!, The
Malihai Clubs Newsletter,
  The
Merlyn's Pen Senior Edition:
  Grades 9–12
Model Railroader
New Era Magazine
Okapi
Partha
Phosphore
Quantum
¿Que Tal?
Radio Control Car Action
react
Sail
Scholastic Action Magazine
Scholastic Art
Scholastic Choices
Scholastic Scope
Scholastic Update
Schuss
Science News: The Weekly
  Newsmagazine of Science

Science World
Scott Stamp Monthly
Skipper
Sky & Telescope
Slap
Spaceflight: The International
  Magazine of Space and
  Astronautics
Straight Magazine
Student Series: Short Story
  International
Surfer
Talents
Teen Beat
Teen Life
Teen Magazine
Teen Power
Teen Times
Teen Voices Magazine
TG Magazine: Voices of
  Today's Generation
360º Magazine
Today in English
TQ (Teen Quest) Magazine
21st Century-Teen Views,
  The
Virginia Writing
Visions
Voices of Youth
Wall Street Journal
  Classroom Edition, The
Weatherwise
Western Horseman
Wild West
Wildlife Conservation
With: The Magazine for
  Radical Christian Youth
WoodenBoat
Workbench
Workbook, The
Writing!
YES Magazine
YM (Young and Modern)
Young Salvationist
Young Scholar
Young Voices
Youth 96
Youth Update
Zelos